Wire as a Weapon

TANK CORPS

AS SEEN BY DON YOUNG, WIREMAN WITH THE TENTH ARMORED DIVISION

TURNER PUBLISHING COMPANY

Turner Publishing Company Staff:
Editor: Erik Parrent
Designer: Herbert C. Banks II

Library of Congress Catalog Card No.
96-60044
ISBN: 978-1-56311-283-6

Limited Edition. Additional copies may be purchased
directly from the publisher.

WIRE AS A WEAPON

With the Tenth Armored (Tiger) Division,
nicknamed the "Ghost Division" by the
Germans because we appeared suddenly
behind their lines, many times.

by
Donald E. Young

Observations of a lineman with the
150th Armored Signal Company laying
wire from 10th Armored Division Headquarters
to the forward units in 1944-45.

FOREWORD

This book was an end result of un-earthing a batch of censored letters sent home to my parents, along with some news clippings saved by my father. This wealth of World War II material either had to be put in a scrapbook, filed or thrown out. You veterans of foreign wars will understand why this memorabilia could not be thrown out!

You can imagine, then, the desire to find out the dates of these various Tenth Armored engagements, and match them up with the writing of 50 years ago. So I sent away to the U.S. Government Archives for the records of the 150th Armored Signal Company and started working on a battle map. Then I was hooked, as I hope you will be!

Don with the 10th Armored in 1944.

The start of this project coincided with my retirement, and became more important than the retirement itself. It became imperative to set the record straight; to give more credit to General Patton than he was getting. Also, the valiant Tenth Armored Division was being omitted in some of the history books because we were loaned out to various armies. We were attached to SHAEF (Supreme Headquarters, Allied Expeditionary Force), as most of you know.

For instance, our Combat Command "B" was sent to relieve Bastogne, made it there in time to block three roads coming in and hold them with about 30 tanks and 500 men each until the 101st came a day later

Complete with Eisenhower Jacket 50 years later.

with their contingent of 10,000. Our men were thankful the 101st came before the town was completely surrounded. They were glad our tanks were there.

Corroboration of dates from the Tenth Armored "Tiger" Division book and our 150th Armored Signal Company history vary by one or two days at most because, depending which combat command we were attached to, from the time we took the town until our wire headquarters caught up was from zero to two days.

TABLE OF CONTENTS

CHAPTER 1
IN THE STATES

After a short few days at Indiantown Gap, for induction into the Army, it was off to Camp Campbell, Kentucky, again by train. So far, it had been a rewarding experience, with a 30-day pass to start. Now we were set for three months of rigorous training. Of course, it started with learning what the letters meant: K.P. stood for something we took turns at doing, unless we went A.W.O.L.; then we would get more than our share of K.P., maybe even some time in the guard house. We looked out for, or looked up to, the O.D. (Officer of the Day) - take your choice which! Finally, the letters K.I.A. - we would get the full impact of that meaning...later on.

It was difficult to get water during chow time, so I learned to drink coffee. One cup was enough, to prevent having to go up for a refill pitcher. "Fall out" meant outside, lined up in our respective squads and platoons. In the morning we had better be dressed in fatigues or in the uniform of the day, with foot-lockers ready for inspection. Guns had to be oiled and ready to present, and we needed to know how to "break down" our firearm and put it together as fast as possible. We also found out that a good way to get K.P. duty was to "break out" laughing during roll call.

Only after several weeks could we apply for passes, if there was no "white glove" inspection or barracks scrub-down. I often thought these duties were designed to keep more G.I's in camp during the weekends to make the camp commander look good if upper echelon brass happened to stop in.

My one overnight pass during basic training was to Nashville, Tennessee. Two girls we met at the U.S.O. dance stopped for us the next evening at the Y.M.C.A., where we stayed, and drove us to the Grand Old Opry. When the bass player's hat somehow fell inside his bulky overalls, we laughed coarsely, but the girls didn't think it was all that funny. It came off OK, since all we had to drink was soda obtained at the corner restaurant where we ate dinner. It was a Southern Hospitality weekend, thanks to Peggy Watts and her friend.

Basic training meant that all GI's had to try for the norm, or average. It was easy if you were in shape! If you thought of training as a series of competitive sports the days went faster and even the rope swing over a mud pit may be taken lightly -that is, if you landed on your feet! It was important to stay on your feet, especially while running the obstacle course from log to log when they're set at various heights like pilings; spaced sporadically like pebbles on a beach.

Crawling through the mud while cradling a rifle in your arms was OK, except before "graduation," when we did it to the tune of overhead machine gun fire. "Keep your butt down," yelled the sergeant, "that's live ammunition." In order to make things more realistic, someone had a sadistic notion to water down part of the course, especially where we swung over a ditch.

I liked the wall we had to climb over, in the obstacle course. A good running start was necessary to get partway up the smooth board surface to maintain momentum for an arm lift at the top. It was quicker to throw a leg over while balanced on straightened arms than to try to force a leg over while precariously hanging on to the edge. The trick was to roll over the edge, do a flip or partial flip, and come down with a push out to a running position.

Of course, there was a modicum of danger in almost everything. For instance, we learned to fall to a prone position with our rifles ready to fire. For Signal Corps personnel the issue was carbines, which were smaller than the M1 rifles. We were instructed to put much of our weight on the butt of our rifles, and occasionally the stock would split, causing sharp splinters to appear close to your face. Breaking the stock was more of a possibility for the larger men, who had to learn to do a barrel roll...knees...stomach; then the rifle butt.

The Army worked as a functioning unit...and my first proof of that, during three months of basic training, was to watch what happens when one person does not adjust to the norm. We had a fellow in our barracks who refused to take a shower. The man on the bunk above him, and the two soldiers on either side, were trying to get him to wash. I was lucky to be three bunks down the line, but the odor was noticeable that far away! Finally, the five who were closest took him into the shower, where there was room for a dozen or more men. The time for pleading was over! They gave him a G.I. bath...complete with soap and stiff-bristle brush that we used to scrub down the barracks floor. After that, everything was back to normal and there was no more odor. I guess there was no more problem with him taking showers...it couldn't be any more embarrassing than what had already happened!

Moving materials was easy with the coordination of many strong backs, working in shifts. Teams from several barracks lifted boxes together to load a couple of boxcars in one night. We learned to flip the boxes to have them land on the side, but eased them down...easier than straight lifting, but still requiring stomach muscles (and strong boxes). Our barracks was the first in line, and I think we were the first ones asleep after we were dismissed.

Sergeants led us on forced "training" marches, with a view to toughening leg muscles...and most any other muscle that moved. At this time I was pressed into service as part of the medical team, perhaps because I had been attending Amherst College as a pre-med student. Bob Bogardus and I were lucky enough to have to carry 20-lb. first aid kits in addition to a full field pack. We mainly treated blisters, with as many as 20 men lined up at the halfway break. From my Scouting experience I knew how to let out the pus by inserting a needle through the skin at the edge (not in the blister itself). Then I applied a one-inch piece of tape directly over the flattened blister. For an open wound, salve was used to prevent further friction, but a bandaid put too much pressure on the sore and took longer to heal. Ten years of track had added to my "blistering" background, but this wasn't on my Army record.

Men would sometimes become overcome by the excessive heat; or become dehydrated because they wanted to pack light, and so didn't bring their canteen. Either way, Bob and I would fade back, away from the dust of the column's rear which fluctuated back and forth. We would administer smelling salts to revive them. Invariably, they were still weak. When the pick-up jeep came up from its dust-free position behind, we would help them in, then run to catch up to the main body. We weren't allowed to ride in the jeep, which ended up with a few men who couldn't finish the hike. Most of them were dehydrated. Next time they would be certain to drink their water!

At the end of such a hike, Bob and I revived two soldiers, helped them into the jeep, then had to jog for about five minutes. By the time we caught up, the platoon had already reached the barracks. Long-legged Bob didn't even seem tired, but I was puffing so hard I failed to notice who was in back of me. "Glad that's over," I said with a twisted grin. Bob laughed "The worst is yet to come." He had seen our Medical Corps Doctors ready with long needles. "Pull up your sleeves and drop your pants," they said. Our laughs turned to groans of dismay as we were hit with a vaccination and two shots, one where we wanted to sit down. In addition to being surprised, it was surprising that Bob and I didn't have any soreness in our arms, or butt, although everyone else we talked to were aching. Guess the extra exertion of running helped our circulation!

As a group we were joined in destiny, to be trained in many different specialties that would make our armies as modern as the moment. I was bound for the Signal Corps...headed for sprawling Camp Gordon, Georgia, home of the Tenth Armored Division.

Hot and sandy, the barracks of the 150th Armored Signal Company became my home of the month. It was catch-up time. The men of the 10th Armored "Tiger Division" were anxious to go overseas. They were ready for two things: to join Patton in Europe as soon as possible, or, if that goal was on hold, to get a pass to nearby Augusta. I listened to talk about equipment: "Some of our new tanks were just sent to Europe - will we follow them, or will replacement tanks be sent to us?" I could tell by the talk that our guys were ready to go, but couldn't find out how soon we would be sent.

Some slots were available for Officer Training School and for the Army Specialized Training School. Bob and I opted for the A.S.T.P., mainly because of our ages. It prooved to be a wise choice, for we were both selected. This was proof enough that our division would be in the states for awhile longer! In a matter of hours we were packed, then waited for a day 'til our orders were ready.

Another train took us to Columbus, Ohio, and Ohio State University, where we were directed to our room in Canfield Hall. Upon arrival, we were told that it was a girls' dorm. That made us a little uneasy, but brought smiles to our faces.

It was formerly a girls' dorm, now with 500 men and one sergeant. With two elevators it was easy to slip out after "bed check", but most who wanted to date during the week would have their bed dummied up so they could get away early. I needed the time to study, which made me chief bed stuffer for my two roommates. It became an art form: for the head, a helmet liner covered partly with a blanket; for one arm, a rolled-up towel bent to look like an elbow; finished off with a couple of pillows to round out the body. Our third

Some of our infantry, with Camp Gordon barracks in the background.

roommate, Irvin X. Goldstein, from Philadelphia, was able to absorb knowledge like a hoagie absorbs sauce. I ended up stuffing his bed several times a week.

We set a time limit of two-and-a-half hours to study before letting anyone in the room. Picture a double bunk on one side, a single cot-like bed on the other, with three desks jammed together in the center, all facing each other. I learned to study during the six months we were at Ohio State, almost eliminating my habit of daydreaming!

With six hours of Physical Education per week it was comforting to have sports available; a lot more fun than taking hikes. Soccer came easy to me because of the amount of running necessary. I was usually able to get to the ball first, tap it to one side, and kick it up-field; but learned the hard way not to kick it with my toes. About the fifth time I tried this trick the opposing player got there first and was standing on the ball. I could hear and feel my toe snap. The gym teacher was not too sympathetic: "I guess that guy was faster than you," he said.

Fortunately, an Army doctor was on call, so I got fast service. I limped into his office in uniform, wearing my "it-doesn't-hurt" smile. "It is probably broken," I said, trying to downplay the whole incident. "It doesn't look too bad," he said, "might be dislocated." With that, he leaned back, pulling on my injured toe. Sweat beaded my face. I guessed the extent of his toe experience was dislocations. I was speechless. He felt the toe again, noticing my pained expression. Then, with a more serious tone: "Maybe we should get an X-ray." Of course, the X-ray showed "fragments widely distributed". I hobbled around the campus for a couple of months.

After six months at Ohio State I was required to return to my division. The toe had healed, and I was in high spirits. Not quite everybody felt good about going back to their outfits. We had two suicides during the six-month period - guys who didn't want to leave, had girls say "goodby" prematurely, or who had trouble keeping up with their studies. We did have a lot of hours of classes... 24, in addition to the six hours of physical education.

My first clue that the division was still on "hold" was when I got a chance to go to the

Girl's dormitories now house units of Army Specialized Training Program.

Shoulder patch of the A.S.T.P.

Army men, bursting out of Converse Hall, form up to march across campus to their next class.

Coeds, Army students, and townspeople jam the stadium at Ohio State to watch a young football team.

Marching student photos from Ohio State Archives.

Radio Operators School at Fort Knox. After just getting back from six months of helping keep the colleges in business, I was off again for another 14 weeks of training.

"We need radio operators," I was told. It was time again to "hurry-up-and-wait." At this school our men could wear their hats on the left, the "armored" way.

It seemed that the Tenth Armored was filling all vacant slots in order to be battle ready. They had evidently discovered that Med Students were available and Pre-Meds couldn't give shots or dispense medicine. I was anxious to get away from being a blister-buster and dive into the radio operator business with exposure to hours of morse code.

The train drummed a sleep-inducing staccato to Fort Knox, Kentucky, which was just as hot as Georgia, but where men ran around with a fervor, bent on learning. It seemed to be part of Patton's Army, which seemed to make the men all the "sharper."

Morse code was taught in groups of words consisting of the same few letters. It was easy to learn small words and then graduate to larger and longer words; finally sentences. We became accomplished with the sounding key, smoothly rolling out the code.

Of course, after each week we tried for a pass, if K.P. or guard duty didn't get in the way. The weather was fine, like Philadelphia on a good Summer day, so I hitchhiked down to the blue grass country to see Calumet Farms. Sitting in the back seat with an older man, I tried not to be upset when he slurred his speech: "Thash my son drivin." We almost pulled out from behind a truck

Sal on the set - while operators rest in the background at the culmination of our training and testing exercises.

This is what our halftracks looked like, except for battle they would sport a 50-caliber machine gun. We later learned to remote the set so it could be operated from inside a building, and still keep it in the track.

at the brink of a hill; got back just in time to avert an accident. When the older woman said "Let's stop at a bar," I declined.

Hoping for a better ride, I ducked behind a tree when they came out, and got a ride soon after. It was fortunate that I hid, because his mother had failed to get him too drunk to drive. I breathed easier when I was finally dropped off at camp in time for "lights out".

After a while we got used to each other's "hand" and could send and receive up to 20 words per minute. Then it was time to take the signal half-tracks out in the field. I wondered why only a couple of recruits volunteered to drive. Someone had told me not to volunteer for anything. In this instance, he was right. I drove for miles while the other men got to send and receive without being rushed, then when we stopped, I sent for a short time, couldn't hear too well, and loused up on the receiving end. "It's time to go back, Young," said the sergeant.

Other men were finishing up their practice in a different type of half-track filled with high-powered radio gear that could latch on to an enemy signal. In conjunction with another track with the same equipment, it could triangulate a position for our artillery or air squadron.

Another train trip landed me back at dusty Camp Gordon on a dreary day when it was difficult to tell whether or not the troops were more active than usual. There was the same talk of readiness, but the place looked the same to me.

C.B. dressed as Monty.

Kief ready for bivouac.

I ended up in a different barracks with the men I would go into battle with - the wire crews. It looked like plenty of exercise to come! Just before all passes were cancelled, the pace of training was stepped up. I was assigned to a wire crew and soon became embroiled in climbing poles. We even practiced on a slanted pole, learning to climb up on the high side. Belting in at the top was the hard part! There were a few problems that could occur if we didn't climb the right way; things that could cause us to fall off a pole. We were told to keep our hooks sharp and our noses clean; in other words, not to clown around. Many of the men were also just learning from those who could run up and down. I soon became adept at climbing methodically. On the ground I could move fast, and after a couple weeks of practice it was almost impossible for me to trip over the wire, but I managed to do it once in a while.

The men had been battle-ready for so long we had started to clown around a little. One very hot day a private challenged the drill sergeant to a race around the parade field - almost a mile, it looked like. It was quite a heated race, in more ways than one; so close I forgot who won!

I do remember having to G.I. the barracks on more than one occasion because of some infraction by one of the men. We all took the rap.

A final week of intensive training featured a day when we only used our climbing belts and weren't allowed to touch the pole. We skidded the belt up the pole, like lumberjacks who climb giant Redwoods, flipping a rope around where they can't reach.

Unfortunately for me, I had trouble keeping my body out away from the pole, which caused my hooks to slip. I burned the pole. Well, that's the right terminology...but actually what happened is that the pole burned me, opening up the back of my knuckles where they grasped the belt. As I started to calmly walk toward the first aid building, the training sergeant said "Go up again, belt in, and look around." Since only the top of my hands were bleeding, it was easy to do, and I tried to be nonchalant about it. I stayed at the top of the pole with hooks and belt in place 'til the sergeant said, "OK - come on down and go over to the first aid station." I felt pretty good about learning, but my knuckles hurt for a couple of days.

Another thing we did that stirred up some excitement was to get some experience holding a hot wire in our hand, or hands. The idea was to eliminate fear of being electrocuted. Of course we were told to be sure to stand on dry ground. We practiced taking 110 volts thru our bodies. After one of the men volunteered to be first to grab the wires, we were anxious to be next in line.

We were all decked out like Bob Anderson, who sought his destiny in Bastogne, literally running wire while shells burst all around, and lived to tell about it. The leggings were found to be a problem. We would doff them along the way to get both mobility and speed.

Hoby could fix anything, especially his jeep, but he learned not to volunteer.

Each man said "Oh, that's easy", but we didn't know if he meant it or not! The sergeant could take 220 volts, but none of us would do that!

The night before the 10th Armored Division left Camp Gordon, it was difficult for me to sleep...not because we were leaving for Europe, but due to the incessant pounding on the headboards. GI's were banging the heels of their hands on their bunks, ostensibly to harden them for battle. The thumping was interspersed with nervous laughter. I tried to sleep, and attributed my difficulty to the noise of other restless men.

With all passes cancelled, we settled down. I had been used to travelling by myself all over the East, but it was good to get to know the men who would be with me for the next eight months. I was closest to Hoby. Happy-go-lucky Hoby who smiled at everything - dust, rain (when we had it), scrubbing the barracks floor (which we all did when someone goofed and wouldn't own up to it); and when he drew K.P. or guard duty. He's the one who had told me not to volunteer, but that was after I got caught. One morning at roll-call our tough training sergeant asked for those who could type. I held up my hand, along with two others. After all, somebody had to dig the ditch, we found out.

Being down in a hole in the hot sun was mild compared to the razzing we endured, questions like: "Are you doing that for fun?" "HOW FAR DO YOU HAVE TO GO TO REACH WATER?" "Are there any rats down there?"..."YOU MEAN ANY OTHER RATS, DON'T YOU?" We got the usual breaks, including a welcome lunch break. After all, we weren't being punished; it just seemed that way! We knew the ribbing was in fun, and it helped to pass the time.

At 19, I was one of the youngest. The Tenth Armored had been in the states for a while, and had a foundation of "older" men. We had followed news of the D-Day invasion and the armored advances into France and wanted to be a part of the battles to come. A lot of new equipment was rolling off the production lines, to link up with the Tenth Armored convoy at the loading docks.

It turned out that we were to be assigned to General Patton as a SHAEF outfit (Supreme Headquarters, Allied Expeditionary Forces). We didn't know it then, but it would mean attacking at different points to give the enemy surprise after surprise.

We were ready. Destiny called.

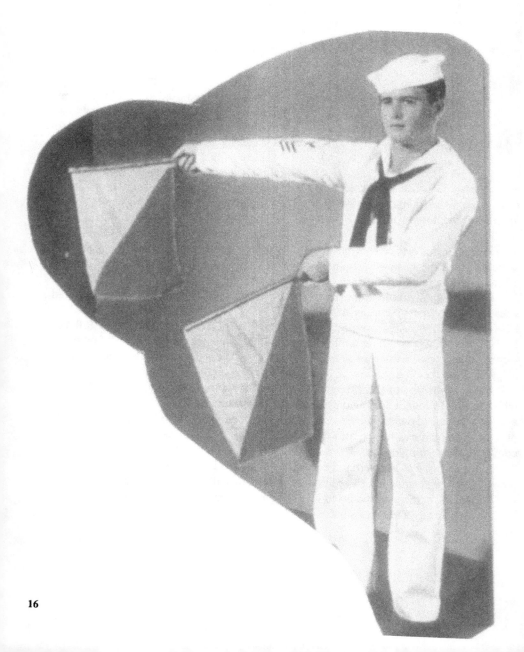

CHAPTER 2
CONVOY

A dreary day greeted us as we lined up on the docks, with a few people waving beyond a roped-off area. Most of us were pumped-up, anxious to get "over there" and do our job. Movement of the troops seemed to come off fairly well, and there was no extra-long hurry-up-and-wait involved as we left the trains and walked to our places on the dock.

When it was time to carry our duffel bags on board the waiting Victory Ship, we shouldered them on our left shoulder, with carbine strap over the right. Encumbered in this manner, it was still possible to salute at the top of the steps, mentioning our names but not the usual permission request. Sergeants were busy with check-off sheets as other companies entered on various gangplanks. Naval officers welcomed the troops on board. A band on the dock played marches.

Below decks it was so crowded with bunks and tiers of narrow hammocks, that I opted to sleep on deck. This turned out to be a wise move, and I was glad to overhear a rumor to the effect that it was O.K. to sleep up there as long as the bedrolls were kept out of the way during the day. I managed to find a corner behind a curved vent pipe about two feet in diameter.

We must have been one of the last ships loaded, for the convoy pulled out with the tide. Ships were scarcely past the harbor when a call came for the first lifeboat drill. We had these drills several times during the zig-zagging trip and never knew when it was for real! Needless to say, our readiness time improved with each drill. We had to run - rather hurry without running - faster each time because the men drifted away from their assigned positions.

Many got seasick, and couldn't hurry as much as they liked. I was glad I had stayed on deck. Below decks there was an almost imperceptible odor, but nevertheless foul. Above decks men lined the rails, trying to reach the water with their meal of an hour before.

A cry went out "look at the sea turtle" but I found my way to the rail blocked by men who were hanging there in a stupor. With a hand over my mouth the mumbled word "MMMMF" seemed to do the trick, and I got to see the huge turtle swimming lazily along. The soldiers at the rail were too sick to notice that I only wanted to see the turtle.

Each company was assigned a specific "mess", so we got used to eating on a schedule. Sometimes it got pretty rough, and plates would slide from one edge of the lipped table to the other. Fewer men would come to eat. So much for small favors. Our Victory, or Liberty Ship wallowed from bow to stern, as well as from port to starboard. The men below thought a storm was in progress. It was just the ship.

Sleek destroyers could be seen on the outer fringe of the convoy, attesting to our meager protection. U-boats must have feared us, however, mostly waiting for a disabled ship to fall behind. Each merchant ship that travelled with our convoys had an Armed Guard of about 30 men, depending on the size of the ship. The merchant ship my friend George Jerram helped guard had eight 20-mm Orlikon's that you had to cock with a cable. After that, the re-coil would throw the next shell into the breech, and they could pump out a barrage for anti-aircraft protection.

According to Jerram, they were sure to man the guns and have them cocked in readiness twice a day, for about an hour and a half at dawn and at sunset. "It is this time of day that the subs would be primed to attack, coming in out of the rising or setting sun," said

Jerram. "One day, when we were releasing the cable off of full cock, one of the men released the spring on the 20-mm gun, but forgot to hook up the cable. The 'twang' could be heard for miles."

His ship also had a four-inch gun on the stern that used armor-piercing shells against submarines. In addition it had a three-inch gun on the bow. "We weren't allowed to fall back to protect a disabled ship. One time (in another convoy) a ship got separated from the convoy due to an engine problem. The captain knew he couldn't ask the convoy for protection, so he tried to keep up, but couldn't, and fell behind the convoy. We looked back and there was smoke on the horizon. The ship was a sitting duck for the waiting submarine!"

Harrison Wymouth Jr., an officer with the Merchant Marine, was also on duty with the First Asst. Engineer of his ship's "black gang," especially when lighting conditions changed. "The subs would attack from the rear, called the 'coffin corner' when the bow gunners couldn't get at them. I was the second man in line, passing up ammo from the hold. It was color coded according to which was needed. We would rendezvous in Halifax Harbor, waiting for ships from various points. Our convoys were primarily to supply the invasion during May of 1944."

We knew that submarines were on the perimeter...even had a boat drill one night. It happened to be a moonlit night and we could see silhouettes of the ships, and figured if we could see them, so could the stalking sub. No great sheet of flame appeared, so it may have been a false alarm.

From our position it was easy to see the outer fringe. Destroyers came up periodically, moving faster than the convoy. If a U-boat appeared, the depth charges could be pumped out, one after the other, set to go off at various depths. The speed of the destroyers prevented them from suffering from the exploding depth charges. Other boats, somewhat smaller, could be seen in between, moving at the same rate of speed as the destroyers. I found out later that they were PCEC's; wooden patrol boats about 40-to-60 feet long. With this ring of depth charge protection, we felt a sense of exhilaration, rather than one of foreboding. It was too far for us to see to the rear of the convoy. We just hoped none of our ships had fallen back where the enemy subs could get at them.

I found out that our subs stayed clear of the convoys because the destroyers, and many other ships, were equipped with racks of depth charges. When the destroyers got a blip on the newfangled Sonar, they would throw out a couple of depth charges. Once in a while we could hear a muffled "poom" as the depth charge exploded beneath the water. We kept staring, transfixed, at the outer ring of the convoy, which was only a couple of rows of ships away. The depth charges looked like 55-gallon drums placed on a slanted rack. We were told to stand clear of them during our drills.

The destroyers had a slanted rack of several depth charges mounted on the starboard side, and another on the port side. "They could throw these depth charges about 50 feet from the ship with compressed air, and set them to go off at different depths. The depths could range from 50 to 300 feet," according to Howard Dorr of our Submarine Service.

"We kept our sub away from the convoy because if we were discovered, it was up to us to get away, and planes would be sent to look for us. If we came up to let them know we were a friendly sub, we would never reach the surface," disclosed Howard Dorr. "Our IFF (Identification Friend or Foe) equipment would conk out after being under water for about a month, and we were often out for two months, sometimes more. The Navy planes could not identify us, so they would drop a bomb or two if they could see where we dove."

Dorr also revealed that their sub hunted Japanese convoys in the Pacific, and also was on "pilot duty" looking for downed pilots who couldn't make it back after a raid. "Sometimes their plane had been shot up and they had to bail out, other times they ran out of gas trying to make it back to the carrier. They sure were glad to see us suddenly appear with no boats around to save them!" said Dorr. "They would be floating there with only a life preserver, worrying about sharks, and didn't care if we were friend or foe.

"We carried 24 torpedoes, plus ammunition for our three-inch bow gun and 40-caliber anti-aircraft gun. Each of us would lose 10 to 15 pounds on a run. The 80-degree South Pacific water was not cool enough to prevent 100-degree temperatures in our sub. The engines and hot electrical equipment did the trick, but when we went to the North Atlantic to help hunt German submarines it was cold. We once had ice forming on the inside of the hull! We were on our own. Even though working in a pack of four subs, we kept 30 to 40 miles apart. That way, there could be no mistake. If we came upon another sub, we knew it wasn't ours," Dorr concluded.

So, as German subs looked for our convoys, we preyed in turn on the enemy U-boats. At the time, we didn't know the enemy subs were having such a difficult time, and we took with a grain of salt the statement "There's nothing to worry about".

The time on board was relegated to a session of calisthenics, followed by a lot of free time. When we weren't assigned to kitchen police, it was easy to get in a game of cards on deck. G.I.'s sprawled all over, playing mainly poker. I would pick my way between the card games until I found four Pennsylvanians playing Pinochle, then wait 'til someone wanted me to fill in. There was plenty of time to wait. Not much time was available for programs because there were too many of us. Even the exercise sessions were cut short when the ship rolled too much, which was at least half the time. I got exercise by getting up early for a couple of laps around the deck before it got crowded. It was seldom jogable. Most of the time I just walked.

One day the ship tilted so much the food trays slipped right off the lipped tables. After this episode, one of the sailors told me to stick a slice of bread under the tray to keep it in place. We became accustomed to grabbing for our coffee or juice. Tables were well mounted so we didn't have to grab at them.

Time was available to write letters home. We were encouraged to do this, especially since some of us were never coming back; although this was never mentioned. The problem was finding the space to write a letter, not the time. This letter, on next page, notes the exact place of origin - somewhere on the ocean. I guess I could have said Atlantic Ocean, although I am not sure that would have been allowed.

One of my requests in the letter was met. Here is the very photo that Dad sent.

The letter also brought to mind the time spent in the hold stacking freight. At the time I remember we had a hollow laugh about it. Up to then neither of us had become seasick, but that was close! To our minds the listing cargo was less dangerous than getting sick. We were buck privates. I remem-

Edna Young.

PASSED BY
U. S.
ARMY EXAMINER

Lt. Howard K. Walls
(CENSOR'S STAMP)

To: MR. AND MRS S. V. YOUNG
320 FARWOOD RD.
PHILADELPHIA 31 PA
U.S.A.

See Instruction No. 2

From: PVT DONALD E. YOUNG
33591041
150TH ARM'D SIG. CO.
A.P.O. 260
c/o Postmaster
NEW YORK CITY
(Sender's complete address above)

Somewhere on the ocean

Dear Folks,

I hope you didn't hurry home from the shore, expecting to see me. No, I didn't know when we would leave. I didn't go anywhere that Friday night. Thought I could get to see Barbara, but no soap. Just before we got on the boat a band played and the Red Cross women gave out coffee and doughnuts. You must get Dad to take a color film of you in your uniform. A sergeant asked Ed and I how we felt and we said "fine" so we were put on a detail and packed boxes in stacks, or stacked them in — well, we worked in the hold all morning and feel fine. The sergeant didn't work and he's seasick now.

Love, "Duck"

HAVE YOU FILLED IN COMPLETE ADDRESS AT TOP?

REPLY BY V···–MAIL

HAVE YOU FILLED IN COMPLETE ADDRESS AT TOP?

ber remarking to Ed: "We can't get any lower than this." He replied, smiling, with sweat on his brow: "Yes we could; the ship could sink." I said "Ha, ha"...but it wasn't a laugh.

After that exchange, we worked feverishly to get the cargo stowed safely, so that we could get out of there, safely. We were breathing heavily, not so much from toil and exertion as from the lack of oxygen down in the hold. Probably the packing cases were absorbing the oxygen; or maybe the air just never got renewed that far down. Great steel ribs curved up the sides of the ship. Above decks, they were hidden by walls, but down here you could see that only the steel hull was between us and the ocean beyond...no insulation, no double hull.

When we reappeared on the deck, job finished, we took large gulps of air. We searched for the sergeant who gave us that duty, but he was off looking for some other soldiers who were not seasick to give them a duty. A corporal crossed our names off the duty roster.

We missed the fresh water showers that, in retrospect, seemed more luxurious compared to the tiny salt water cubicles on board ship. When I took a shower my clothes were kept nearby, just in case a torpedo hit. Lifeboat drills were held several times on the voyage...sometimes because a German U-boat was in the area. Always we tried to get to our stations and complete the boat drill faster than the last time. Actually, we never knew which time would be our last! This tended to speed up our boat drills.

When weather was good, the ship still rolled and men felt too queasy to head for the chow line. I always figured it was better to have a full stomach than an empty one. John Cain, who cooked for 500 men on a Liberty Ship told me that on an earlier convoy they had shot down nine out of twelve German planes that attacked his convoy. Our trip was not as dramatic as this. When I talked to John after the war he said he was at the Rhine preparing for a night crossing when an 88 hit his cook stove and blew it up.

He also related that at Salerno, General Patton was directing traffic at the beachhead while, off-shore, German planes were pounding our ships. At the time we didn't know where Patton was, but were hoping to be assigned to him. His reputation was such that armored personnel wanted to be in his army. I later figured out why General Patton was so much in evidence during an attack. He wanted to make sure that everything went off smoothly.

When our convoy reached England, we stopped overnight, probably to receive navy personnel to make sure we made it directly to the French port of Cherbourg. We were the first convoy to enter the port since sunken ships were removed from the harbor entrance. Spars still poked their way above the surface on either side as our ships snaked their way through in single file. Duffel bags were to be sent separately to our encampment, so we were ready with our packs, bedroll and rifles when it came time to debark.

We soon found out why we left the ship with only part of our gear. With ships jamming the harbor it was necessary to climb down large square-roped landing nets to the waiting barges below. The way they were draped over the side of the ship made it easy to climb down, except for the first step onto the ropes. Spotters stood by to help us over the side. Here's where our obstacle course training came in handy!

The Navy was on hand again. They ferried back and forth in large flat-bottomed barges, bringing thousands to shore. It was an experience rather than an ordeal. After many monotonous days at sea we were anxious to get on shore and put up our pup tents in the fog, mist and rain to come.

CHAPTER 3
GETTING READY FOR BATTLE

My induction came as a result of a letter from President Roosevelt, but many of us became interested in the U.S. Army as a result of ads like this one from the U.S. Army Recruiting Service:

JOE STARTED WITH A JALOPY...

"Up to his elbows in grease and surrounded by a backyard full of spare parts, the teen-age jalopy genius has become an important American tradition.

"American young men know a lot about the insides of engines. Usually they've spent hours stripping the old jalopy down to nuts and bolts and putting it together again.

"The U.S. Army has machines that make an automobile look as simple as a thimble, but the man who picked up a knowledge of mechanics in his own backyard can learn to make them work - with ease.

"The tanks, trucks, bulldozers and mobile armor that make up our fast-starting, hard hitting Ground Forces open new vistas for the man who likes to know what makes things go.

"Maintenance is the background of a Mechanized Force. The U.S. Army is constantly engaged in finding new and better ways to keep 'em rolling. Army vehicles are well cared for because the men who keep them in shape are trained for the job!

"The tanks and armor which spearhead ground attacks are the best equipped and maintained in the world. The American soldier moves forward with confidence - he leads the advance in ground-eating giants.

"The modern Army is a laboratory and testing ground for the latest engineering developments, and its soldiers are in on the ground floor of progress. They see tomorrow's improvements today - in an outfit where new twists are commonplace.

"Today thousands of young men are choosing the Regular Army life. The Army offers unexcelled schools for training in over 200 trades and skills, a world-circling variety of assignments, and a rich opportunity for men who want to launch interesting and useful futures.

"Any qualified, physically fit young man, from 18 to 34 inclusive (17 with parents' consent), may enlist in the new Regular Army. Increased pay, excellent food and quarters, and the chance to advance make the Army one of the finest careers open today. Ask for details at your nearest Army Recruiting Station."

No barracks for us this time! We pitched pup tents in a field...rows of them with "streets" in between that became mud paths in the rains of Normandy. The weather induced me to dig out my own rectangular poncho from my duffel bag a day later, when our bags arrived from the ship. Using that as a ground cloth, I could wear the Army issue poncho, which was less cumbersome to wear, but would not cover the grass and mud beneath my blanket roll. This is one time my varied camping experience paid off. At other places along the way, where we had to use our tents, our crew obtained permission to set them at angles.

Much of our equipment arrived during the first few days. It evidently had been stashed somewhere on one of the ships in our convoy. We waited for some, but many of the jeeps and halftracks were new, and it took us a while to outfit them, taking turns with welding equipment.

Our wire reels had to be mounted on "A" supports so they could spin off wire as we drove down the road. We also attached a vertical piece of steel to the front bumper, extending it above the height of the windshield. A small forward-slanting strip at the top would prevent piano wire, strung across the road, from riding up and over the hood to catch us in the face when we drove with the windshield down.

Then off we went, "marching" to the front, with everyone riding; all on wheels or treads. All armored divisions were mechanized so that everybody had a vehicle to ride in. Our crew had a halftrack and a jeep, both with wire reels on welded A-frames. As we moved further East into France I saw one of the first extensive bombing raids - planes from horizon to horizon in all directions. B17s on their way to pay their respects to Berlin, plowing through bursts of flack. One of the planes started to drop its bombs. A bomb fell a mile away. "Guess the Lutwaffe got that B17," Hap commented, craning his neck, looking taller than ever. "How many bombs in a stack?" asked Frank, as another one exploded a half mile closer. In unison we ran, looking for a foxhole.

While we were scurrying to avoid the misplaced bombs, we missed some fancy dog-fights that were taking place above the bombers as hundreds of our fighters tried to protect the larger planes. The Luftwaffe lost a lot of their remaining Air Force that day!

I found a muddy shallow crater which my buddies passed up. Every time a bomb hit, I flattened out and my chest dipped into the mud. I did about three muddy pushups before the bursts faded into the background of roaring engines. I came up laughing. My two friends were laughing at my mud-splashed face; I chuckled at how they looked as they scampered for cover, searching for a dryer hole. Hap had jumped over the fence, like a hurdler, while Frank was going under, between the rails. They made a bizarre silhouette on this memorable day.

Frank laughed so much he was speechless, which was unusual for him. He was particularly adept at discussing weighty issues of the world...without going into an argumentative mode. I was more opinionated, but Frank could lead us all to a conclusion, although not necessarily the one he started with. On the outcome of the war, we all agreed. We would win.

Frank and I were usually the first ones up in the morning and would wake our crew chief. He always wanted to get an early start, even before the password of the day was given to us by Division Headquarters. Not knowing the password got us in trouble on a regular basis. We had to be careful when approaching another unit...not to be quick with our motions.

An interesting aspect of the French countryside was the roadside farms we passed during the days to come. Each farm was complete with adjoining square stack of hay, layered with cow manure; close between the house and the pump. As far as we

Frank Armbuster at the Camp Gordon Barracks.

were concerned, it was a little too close. We favored the quaint farm outbuildings for sanitation over warmth.

For water, we tried to pick places where the pump was separate from the hay/manure heap, or wait for the water truck to come up!

My first glimpse of French hedgerows occurred in the dampness of dusk as we scooted toward the East. We learned Patton's marching orders; when a tank or other vehicle got stuck along the sloping shoulder of a road made muddy by skidding treads it was to be pushed aside by another tank, or dozer, if one was available. Lessons learned on the mountain roads of Italy were repeated on muddy lanes in France.

We had a lot of faith in our officers and sergeants, many of which had been trained by Patton personally at his desert training center. His imprint was left on all who followed. Patton refused the semi-deluxe quarters at the small, dusty town in the desert area, insisting that his officers also forgo using the town as their accommodations. In contrast, Monty's suite in Gisa, next to the Pyramids, was in a good hotel with a view of both Pyramids and the Sphinx.

Patton was also to thank for our most effective radio equipment. He originally purchased radio equipment out of his own money to equip troops at the Desert Training Center. This set the stage for communication to the tanks. He felt it was important to be able to reach the troops in seconds in order to save time in training. Though he was tough on his troops, he was also tough on himself and shunned the niceties that some officers feel are necessary to get their troops to look up to them. Patton was the kind of man his troops had confidence in!

General Patton was known for leading his troops. Ray Wilson, a tank commander with the Seventh Armored Division, observed that, "Patton was never in the back of the ranks; he was always up front yelling 'come on, come on' to his men. If five of our tanks were knocked out just to get one German tank, Patton didn't care." Ray's positions in the tank were gunner, driver, and tank commander. He was never a loader, but always a leader.

Gunners received $65.00 per month; tank commanders $80.00 a month, but they had to stick their head out of the tank to look around. Some would do this even during a battle. They could not see much using the tank's scope.

The 10th Armored landed in France, but the 7th Armored had been running secret maneuvers with their tanks, in England, and were not even stationed in a specific area. They were billeted in several towns, and never trained during the day. The tanks had powerful lights, flashing red, green and orange, with which they hoped to blind the Germans 300 yards away. There was just a slide that the light shone through. The tankers could shoot through the slide and then close it to avoid retaliating machine gun fire. The reason we didn't use this trick more often must have been the feasibility of lining up a bunch of tanks without alerting enemy artillery.

We followed into battle almost in the numerical sequence of our armored divisions. Later on, when the 10th Armored was approaching the Rhine in the southern sector, the 7th Armored was crossing on a pontoon bridge at Aachen. These special lights on Ray's tank helped him spot German frogmen trying to blow up the bridges.

This was one of the few times our specially-equipped Sherman tanks were able to effectively use their lights. They lined up a row of tanks to illuminate the entire bridge. The trick was to maintain about 30 yards between tanks to present a wall of light; which proved effective thanks to tactics learned in the 18,000 sq. mile Desert Training Center.

The Training Center booklet explains the LDC arc lights, nicknamed after the "Canal Defense Light Project" because, in World War I, a Royal Navy Commander proposed use of a searchlight mounted on a tank to blind the enemy. Like our government, the British War Office twice turned down the idea, but eventually it was adopted in the 1930's.

"When the M-4 Sherman tanks replaced the M-3 General Lee/Grant tanks in the western desert in 1943, it was decided to convert some of the spare Grant tanks to CDL configuration. It was determined that the conversion could easily by made and the Grant had the advantage of having its 75mm gun mounted in a sponson for offensive action.

"To accommodate the CDL configuration, the searchlight turret was divided into two compartments. The operator sat on the left and operated his equipment which was located on the right side of the turret. The 13 million candlepower light came from carbon-arcs mounted in the center and through various reflectors the light passed through a vertical slit to hit the target horizontally. The reflectors were made of polished aluminum which prevented the mirror from being shattered by machine gun or small arms fire. In fact, it was found that the light's intensity was hardly affected even after repeated hits."

In addition, the slit could be opened and closed six times a second with an automatic device, and various colored filters made it difficult for the enemy to determine the range. When the lights were tested in the open, officers assigned to the project couldn't tell how far away the tanks were!

Every day we passed vehicles bogged down along the road. We had to coordinate a toss of wire still attached to the mounted reel by throwing it over the tank turret like swinging a lasso. Then up we went, up a pole or tree, digging into the slippery surface with our hooks, belting in so we could remove wet gloves to tie the line on pole top or cross-arm. I would use a clove hitch at the top of a pole, being careful not to run out of pole where my hands would go.

One evening I was literally up a tree without a password. I had one leg over a branch in order to fix a line broken by a tank antenna at the entrance to their field. Suddenly, in the gloom of approaching night, a tanker appeared below with his "grease gun" open, ready to shoot. "What's the password?" he said nervously. I mumbled "MMMFFW"...then realized I had been holding a glove in my mouth - quickly spat it out and yelled "How do you expect me to know the password when I've been out all day laying wire!"

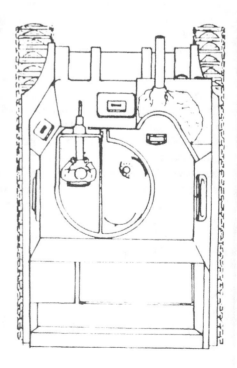

That seemed to do the trick. Sometimes, it wasn't that easy. Four of our crew were out on the division flank one day, looking for a string of telephone poles with good wire that we could tap into to reach the town up ahead. We waved to a group of G.I.'s ahead of us, and proceeded to head for the nearest pole. Suddenly, we noticed the multiple 50, mounted on the back of a halftrack. It was swinging our way, aiming for our man on the pole. I almost blurted out "nicht", when I realized we had contacted the French

Second Armored on our flank. They were outfitted with our equipment. We approached with caution, replying to their French with a couple of French words and letters like U.S.A. When they smiled, we still weren't sure we were safe because the 50-caliber machine guns continued to point in our direction, and the French Morrocan troops had filed their teeth to points, which made their smiles sinister indeed. At various times, the French 2nd Armored was on our right flank. We hardly ever ran into divisions beside us. We went as far as headquarters of our battalions on the flank.

They had been on our flank since Paris, where we had swung past the Arc de Triumph at the tail of our convoy. A steady rain was making driving difficult for me (Hoby was driving the lieutenant). With one hand I had to move the windshield wiper from left to right and also keep an eye on our crew sergeant, who was catching up on his sleep. As we turned a corner, his head lolled to the right and his helmet fell out of the jeep. I braked to a stop, nudging him inconspicuously: "Ellya - wake up - get your helmet." He jumped out, retrieved his helmet and was back in the jeep just as our lieutenant came up from his vehicle. "What's the trouble?" he scowled. "No trouble, sir," I said. "We just hit a bump and his helmet fell out."

We camped out to the North of Paris, skirting the Champs Elysees while the French Second Armored paraded through, then broke camp to continue the "march". General DeGaulle had marched down the avenue once before, in August, when the Allies liberated the city on the Seine. The arrival of November found us sleeping in old buildings. A pot-bellied stove warmed the room when we could find one, while we came in and out from our duties repairing bomb-broken lines. In a letter to my parents I wrote: "The line is out again so I don't expect to be back 'til midnight." It was usually much later if we had to go out on night duty. I just wanted to present a normal work routine to the folks at home.

An overhead break in the wire is found by scanning it with a stare against the night sky while standing up in the jeep; sometimes wasting an hour or more until the moon comes out enough for us to see the wire. It is not advisable to turn on headlights, so the windshield remains flipped down. Flashlights are used sparingly only when we are following wire on the ground. Overhead the nightly flight of "Washing Machine Charlie" sputtered ominously back and forth, searching for a target to give to the enemy planes that come out in the night like termites. No tracers were aimed at this spotter plane, so as not to give away their positions below.

Up ahead a front is developing - and I don't mean weather. The day before our first action happened to be Sunday and I got a chance to go to church out in a field, where we received communion and said a certain amount of prayers.

An idea of the fervor that was lavished on General DeGaulle was in evidence at a small town where we parked bumper-to-bumper on the main street, waiting for the signal to move ahead. French people shouted and waved, and passed coffee laced with bourbon directly from their windows to our vehicles. They leaned out over the narrow sidewalk to reach our halftrack. We had caught up to the tanks to participate in this welcome. It was one of those quaint, backroad towns our Command happened to cover.

This took place in the vicinity of Mars la Tour, France, our first action on November 2, 1944. It was fitting that we have this kind of reception. We knew this was a war to rid the world of an evil, namely, suppression of freedom...but it gave us a good feeling to be appreciated by the very people we are liberating. One of General Patton's remarks that week was that the Tenth Armored was moving into battle in good order.

Nightfall found us bedded down in our pup tents near town. We are introduced to the sound of artillery in the distance, lulling us to sleep. It would not be anything to worry about; it was just there. Closer brushes with the symphony of incoming and outgoing shells would follow, and we would learn the size of a shell by its tone.

Early in the morning it was again time for wire. We were up at dawn because we knew that the tanks were going to engage the enemy and everyone wanted the wire to be in place. For the next few days, as we approached Metz, we laid more wire than ever; 300 miles of it in three days! One thing we had was good communication, a strongpoint of Patton's personal involvement with the early training of his armored divisions. His own division formed the cadre for those to follow.

We began to see dead cows and horses, swollen so much that their legs stuck out at an awkward angle, higher than horizontal. I put two and two together. If they had a putrid odor, the battle had passed through here some time ago! The less people we saw, the greater the resistance must have been.

When the Germans left before our troops arrived, the townspeople would stay. If the Germans prepared to defend the town, most of the civilians would leave. Some would hide in basements. By the time we got to the towns, the French would be back again, or we would meet them on the highway. They had played hide-and-go-seek with artillery and were on their way back to claim their homes. Advance troops often-times made a shambles of the place. In those instances it would be deserted and at least we could find a building to bed-down in. We were always too tired to make an effort to clean. Even Frank, who was probably the most fastidious, just pushed the rubble aside.

On the outskirts of these towns there were demolished buildings, if not throughout town. My friend Lt. Hemcher, from the 741st Tank Battalion explained it this way: "We found that the Jerrys were knocking off our tanks from hiding places in haystacks and garages on the edge of towns. After that we would blast haystacks and garages as we came into a town." That must have been tough on the little farms, most of which had a haystack up against the house.

Beyond Mars la Tour the Tenth Armored raced for the city of Metz. German troops were already under siege by Allied divisions fighting to pin them up against the wide river. Thousands were captured. Others fought with their backs to the Moselle River. "Leave some for us," our tankers shouted to front-line troops on their way back for more ammunition.

By now, day skies belong to us. However, the Luftwaffe learned to play hit and run, and would strike when our planes were returning from a mission. By the times the planes assigned to Third Army for support had returned to their base to gas up, the German aircraft had vanished over the horizon. They always found enough aircraft to bomb the bridgeheads, although multiple 50's anti-aircraft guns managed to knock a few enemy planes out of the sky each time the Krauts tried to blast one of our bridges.

Combat Command "A" passed through Nancy, and it may have been two of our cooks in the photo to the right by the U.S. Army Signal Corps. You can see the place where the armored division triangle has been removed from their arms. Men of the Tenth Armored Division, fighting incognito, had removed our patches, as instructed.

Deployment for battle found us eating canned rations at first, but we quickly got in the swing of a powerful armored division on the move. Our cooks took pride in furnishing hot meals at the drop of a tailgate. All the wiremen got hot meals more often than not, except when we got in too late for the cooks to break out the supplies that were all loaded up ready to pull out for the next town. Sometimes we were all loaded up ready to go at daybreak. Maybe then we wouldn't even get a hot breakfast. I'm sure the infantry pitied us.

Between the cities of Nancy and Metz, the 80th Infantry Division softened up the Germans. John Richardson of Co. "E" relates his experience when his infantry platoon ran into some German tanks that were blasting them from a nearby hill and had them pinned down. "Our armored recon tanks were called back to support us, but there were only three of them and one was stuck in the mud. Night was approaching, so we had anti-tank guns brought in and put in place. In the morning, as soon as it was light, our observers saw the German tank crews having breakfast and we were able to cut loose with these guns. After two of the enemy tanks were knocked out others left their camouflaged positions and took out over the hill. The anti-tank guns then shot at them like in a shooting gallery, and when we moved up there were knocked out tanks all over the place. Only two escaped."

Later on, the 80th was rolling along, but Richardson was wounded while attacking in the fog. He lay there in a fog and in the fog, unnoticed until about an hour into the battle. "A buddy coming back with prisoners saw me and had the prisoners carry me on one of their overcoats," relates Richardson. "When it started to split, they kicked off a door from a nearby outbuilding, all the time guarded by this G.I. from one of our other platoons. I guess they were in a hurry to reach a safe place, too! They hurried back, with me on the

door. I was flown across the channel to England to a chest center where Colonel Tourhof, from Battle Creek, Michigan, took out the bullet."

Meanwhile, according to Patton's plan, an engineering battalion attached to the 90th Infantry Division was moving up their bridge-building troops, along with sections that really looked like a bridge. Half of our division crossed on this Bailey bridge, the rest of us would move over the pontoon bridge.

As soon as Twentieth Corps knew that the 90th Division had established a bridgehead at Thionville and were building a bridge over the flooded Moselle, the 10th Armored was rushed to Rumelange to wait for an opportune time to cross. It was a small town some miles back from the river so we could lay in wait like the tigers that we were. The town had met our tanks on November nine. Five days later we would move over two bridges, more than ten thousand strong.

On November 15, CCA started over an undulating pontoon bridge already under fire. Overhead, shells from long-range 155's of the 30th Infantry Division whistled from the rear to drive back the German guns. Our wire track was always next to last in line when Combat Command "A" took the rear position. We had a good view of Jeeps and trucks of Division Headquarters moving across the bridge ahead of us, and we could see tanks in the distance, crawling off into the mist. We couldn't see the other side of the bridge, and what at first looked like mist turned out to be smoke. By the time our team crossed it was

General Patton crossing the Seine River on August 26, 1944 on a bridge composed of dozens of pontoons strung side-to-side. Engineers are still checking the guy wires. (Courtesy of Patton Library.)

The famous airhorns on General Patton's jeep meant, "Move aside to let me get to where the action is."

very late in the day. Engineers had kept smoke pots going to hide the bridge from probing artillery and possible air attack.

We heard mostly outgoing artillery, since the 90th Infantry Division had established a bridgehead and had the Germans on the run. South of us, the 5th Infantry Division was encircling the city, while the 95th attacked it head on. Our part would be important in preventing any reinforcements from arriving at Metz from the North. An armored division was ideal for this assignment because we could move to our position in a hurry and we did!

One company of our 132nd Ordnance had a wrecker stationed at the bridge in case they had to remove a vehicle stranded due to break down or bursting shells. They followed along behind Combat Command "A" as soon as we cleared the shore-line.

Crossing the Moselle at Thionville on a pontoon bridge too long to see to the other end seemed a flimsy thing to do, considering our wire track weighed nine tons, plus a double rack of wire along one side. Then I recalled that tanks must have gone before, so I relaxed and looked ahead instead of at the flexing guy wires.

The crossing behind us, we headed into battle. It was a long "march" that lasted 'til after dark. Unfortunately, the maintenance halftrack had trouble with their motor, so we dropped back to give them support if they would need it. The sky was black on a moonless night when we started off again to find the rest of our outfit. Hesitating at a fork in the road, we went left. A mile or so down the lane it began to look very woodsy, and I happened to see tracers up ahead like dotted lines arching across the road. Evidently no one else saw them, even though Hap was on the 50-caliber just in case. "Tracers up ahead," I yelled, banging on the cab roof. With that, Pug swung the 'track' around, while we motioned to the maintenance track behind us. When Frank pointed to the road ahead, and then to our machine gun, they caught on at once and followed us out of there!

What surprised me was the fast way my buddies responded, since I was the youngest in the crew. It was not a time for lengthy discussions, so we headed back to the fork in the road and took the right hand road to find our outfit. Our track was really rolling so we kept an eye on the maintenance vehicle behind us to make sure they maintained the pace. We finally got to our bivouac area more than an hour after the rest of the Tenth. We had closed the back door to Metz.

It was easy to lay wire across a bridge. If it was a bridge with any kind of pontoons, we just drove over and flipped the wire out onto the floats, making sure to tie it at both ends so it wouldn't sag between the pontoons. A Baily or trestle bridge afforded places to tie the line, looping it from one vertical support to another. In any case, we got across the bridges as fast as possible so as not to hold up traffic...or attract fire.

It was more difficult to get through the towns. One way was to use existing lines. Later on, when we got more entrenched in Thionville, France, lines for our Twentieth Corps were patched into the main city switchboard.

CHAPTER 4
ACROSS THE MOSELLE

We were fairly fresh but were getting used to incoming shells, which didn't bother us much because usually they were just searching, and didn't really have a bead on us. Frank was proud that the bursts didn't bother him, and when I called him 'fresh' in jest he just put on an imaginary scowl...his Patton look, he called it. Even though we were supposed to be with SHAEF as a reserve division, we thought of ourselves as Patton's armor.

We hoped we would live up to General Patton's requirements, and maybe not get killed doing so. In his speech to his men, given in England, he told this story: "One of the bravest men I ever saw in the African campaign was one fellow I saw on top of a telegraph pole in the midst of furious fire while we were plowing toward Tunis. I stopped and asked him what the hell he was doing up there at that time. He answered, 'Fixing up the wire, sir.' 'Isn't that a little unhealthy right now?' I asked him. He answered, 'Yes sir, but this Goddam wire's gotta be fixed!' There was a real soldier. There was a man who devoted all he had to his duty, no matter how great the odds, no matter how seemingly insignificant his duty might appear at the time."

All of the various wire teams became very adept at finding a break in the line. We worked in pairs when we shot trouble - had to notice things that would lead us to the damaged wire, no matter what time of day it was. We learned what to look for, and when. Things like tank tracks or the mark of skidding howitzers being towed into a field. If our line wasn't high enough, the muzzle would tip up and break our wire as the gun dipped out of the roadside ditch on the way to a bivouac in the field. It was easy to climb poles to the top, but not so for trees. Branches would get in the way of the crossing wire, so this line was sometimes placed lower than usual to keep it out of the way of whipping branches that might cause it to break. These were the most difficult kind of breaks to find, because often only one side of the line would be damaged, making it tough to see, especially at night.

One bright sunny afternoon is etched in my mind. The road ran through an open field on the far side of a small riverside town. Trees had been planted in a row on the left side of the road where we wanted to lay wire, but we couldn't climb the 15-to-20-ft. trees, and they were too tall to throw the wire over without two of us handling it. Even Hap, who was steadfast as well as tall, couldn't get it over by himself. We gave a Lawrence Welk one, a-two...on three we tightened the line and snapped it, letting loose immediately afterward. This feat didn't always work on the first try, but we managed to get lines over two trees before the bursting 88 shells started to bother us - and there were about four more trees to go!

Shells were landing near the road about 100 yards away. We finally figured out they were shooting at us, and must have spotted us from up on the hill across the swollen river. One of us got the idea of breaking the inch-diameter trees so we could easily flip the wire over away from tank treads to come. It worked. Three or four of us were able to break the trees and we got to the other side of the field before enemy 88's could get our range.

A day later, when we followed our troops to the next town, we stopped for a moment to wonder how it was possible to snap off these small trees. Did you ever try to break a broomstick over your knee?

Maybe the Germans didn't know what division we were at first, but they sure had a bead on us from up on the Siegfried Line! They had us spotted, but we couldn't see where the shots were coming from. Our division patches had been removed, which is one reason why there was such a mystery surrounding the Tenth Armored. Although the enemy could see the dark triangles on our shoulders where the division patch used to be, it took him a while to determine which armored division he was up against. Sometimes we must have been mistaken for the 6th Armored, on our flank from time-to-time during special campaigns. They were a regular Third Army outfit, and also confused the Germans by their maneuvers. Patton, the father of armored force training in the states, didn't always go by the book. Most of his divisions learned to not go by the book!

Running out the wire was more traditional. We followed wherever the headquarters of our different battalions ended up. As we worked our way into Germany, more often than not our billet for the night was a house, deserted when the civilians ran from our artillery bursts. During the night we shot trouble as the lines themselves were shot by shrapnel from incoming mail. In the morning it was off again, spreading miles of wire.

In some areas, where the front was more "stable", the wire crews expended more wire because they were always under fire and it was safer to roll out another wire than to fix the breaks. Also, it took less time. Sometimes wire had to be picked up when the troops moved on, in order to have enough for the next campaign. Troops in the photo below may have just completed the tedious job of winding up wire. Note the handle.

While we were billeted to the rear of Metz, some of our units ended up fighting in the city; so we faced the city, and also faced on a daily basis, enemy soldiers in small towns to the North of the city. They were hunkered down either as a division or as parts of divisions. Some of them did not give up easily, especially the Germans in Metz. For most of them it would be the river of no return.

A lot of these units stationed in the small towns must have been fed a stream of lies about what we would do to them when or if they were caught. At any rate, they would fight to the end. We could surprise them, or outsmart them, but once the fight was under-

way they were very stubborn, and had to be persuaded by a superior show of arms that actually blew them away. Then, sometimes, their comrades would come out. Once we had knocked out their 88's it was easier to get them to surrender. The best coercion was a couple of hand grenades lobbed into a window. The survivors would come out.

It is my opinion that our grenades were more effective than theirs, at the end of a stick! Our men could lob them farther with our baseball experience. We could carry more in our pockets or hung by the pins, as many were wont to do...and our men didn't have that handle to contend with to get in the way when they tried to throw a grenade through a pillbox slot or a window.

Even small towns would wreak havoc with our advance when there was a good defense. We had to clean them out one house at a time. Tanks would blast the machine gun nests as they went through, hoping they would also get enemy bazookas. At the end of one of these towns we could hear machine gun fire as we approached the near end of town...the town we were supposed to lay wire to! Our infantry had disembarked and was smashing through, grenade after grenade. We could hear the low throbbing sound of a BAR and the faster staccato of the German machine guns.

Since it was early in the day it looked like we might have to go on to the next town, a few miles down the road. Fields around town were mud-filled so Sgt. Ellya said, "Take it right down the main street." That meant stringing the wire from one window to the next. Maybe this town had wire underground, but it didn't look modern enough for that. Houses three stories high stood side-by-side in rows.

One of us had to go up to the third floor to catch the loop, so two of us went up each time, carrying our guns at the ready. We never knew when there might be some of the enemy hiding out in the upstairs rooms.

This sketch shows how we threw a double coil of wire so it would reach to the third floor, or to a high tree limb. This method proved easier than tying a weight on the end, which, in itself, took a lot of time. The line created too much drag to throw up a single coil. With this double-coil method we could reach the third floor sometimes on the first try!

ATTACK AT DAWN

Oh, what wondrous webs
We weave, of wire...
Keeping up with treads
Of tanks, in mire;
Where they cut across
To by-pass eighty-eights,
Where German troops have lost.

A speeding tank creates,
Where once the muddy water flows,
These emptied pools of mud
That splash on wiremen's clothes.

The widening river, soon to flood,
Will make these puddles full again
And tanks take on a new direction.

Nightly freezing pools and sleeting rain
Disturb the engineers where bridge erection
Will continue all night long
As spearheads come from South and North,
Confirming, with the coming dawn
That daybreak sends our Army forth;
Though engineers have worked all night
To help insure our armored clout...
To let our men control the fight
And bring to head the German's rout.

General Morris, left, and General Patton, right, look over 10th Armored bridge just completed by our engineers over an unnamed river, one of many we crossed. (Courtesy of Patton Library.)

Our armored infantry was also starting to come in contact with mine fields, mines set in the mud on the back roads, and even the wire crews had to look out for bouncing bettys when we laid wire out around a field. When a trip wire was hit, the small anti-personnel mine would spring up in the air and then explode.

Patton didn't recommend that infantry advance through a mine field without clearing it, but he did mention that a division that did it at night lost about 35 men, and that if they had done it under fire in the daytime they would have lost the same 35, plus up to 200 to machine gun fire. The Russian troops cleared mine fields that were in their way by advancing infantry without regard for mines, night or day!

Two other kinds of bridges: Top: Bailey bridge built under fire by 1340th Engineer Battalion near Trevieres, France. Just Above: Treadway Bridge built by "A" Company, 254th Engineer Battalion over Aure River. (Courtesy of Patton Library. Oakes photos)

CHAPTER 5

BEYOND METZ - THE SIEGFRIED LINE

When we joined the battle it was not to replace another division. It was to enter into the fray - that's what Patton had planned for us, anyway! When Patton planned to leapfrog, he seldom had one division falling to the rear and another replacing it; he alternated infantry and armor. We spearheaded many drives where infantry would follow for miles...and other attacks that necessitated that the foot soldiers come up on the town while our whole division scooted around to outflank the enemy, cutting through the German division with a swath of tanks. We found out later that we could do this because General Patton knew where to place his tank divisions!

When the war started there was one warring nation and a lot of surprised peaceful ones. Now the Germans were losing - and it was no surprise to us. It was understandable, for instance, that the deer hunters from our Pennsylvania 28th Division would be a major threat to the Krauts. Even though they bore the brunt of Panzer attacks, thereby sustaining many casualties, the final figures show that the troops they fought against had twice as many losses in spite of tanks to help them! Divisions that supported our armor, or led the way at times, also had many mountain men who could bark a squirrel if put to the test! A lot of us fired BB guns, twenty twos or 30-30's in the process of growing up, and could hit the mark whether we were professional soldiers or not.

Days were getting colder, but roads remained mud-streaked from the tanks that etched tracks from shoulder-to-shoulder. I would take damp or soggy socks off at night so my feet would be dry in the blanket bag, getting warmth by pressing them together. My "bag" would stay together because I had brought three-inch blanket pins from home, using them to maintain a French pleat at the edges. Many of my friends would never want to go camping again after their experiences in World War II. I didn't feel that this was camping. It was just an interlude in our lives where we endured cold, wet and muddy conditions, with danger thrown in.

One time we had five of our bedrolls in a row in a room in a vacated house that must have featured a dog. We were there for two nights. The first night the first two men announced that fleas had attacked their blankets. The rest of us laughed while they sprinkled DDT in their bedding, then the second night the third man started scratching, and you should have seen us shake the DDT. When I hear the James Bond line 'shaken, not stirred' it brings to mind that night.

We carried the Carbine, but I noticed the infantry that accompanied us, men of the 30th, all carried the larger M1 rifles. They all had their bayonets, and had occasion to use them from time-to-time. Our Armored Infantry also used the M1 rifles, and kept their bayonets sharpened. Patton, in his special instructions, stressed that "Few men are killed by the bayonet; many are scared by it. Bayonets should be fixed when the fire fight starts. Bayonets must be sharpened by the individual soldier. The German hates the bayonet and is inferior to our men with it. Our men should know this."

G.I.'s hung grenades on their belts by the pins, so they didn't have to take two hands to throw one. There was always a difference of opinion on how to safely handle it. Some men opted for a slight edge by being quicker; others thought more carefully of the danger when they didn't need the grenades.

The Twentieth Corps used our division according to Patton's system. We were evidently using the 'back door' philosophy; preventing the enemy from escaping to the North.

We certainly did that. We got behind his lines and started to take prisoners in the Saar-Moselle triangle.

Our men would ride to a town, jump off the tanks, fight thru the town and go on to the next. Here at the Siegfried Line, infantry of the 90th Division had been in the line keeping the enemy at bay for weeks. Sometimes, when men of a supporting infantry division arrived, walking, they were told the front was six miles further. Then the accompanying infantry division's men would cast slurring remarks at our "riding" infantry, mostly in jest.

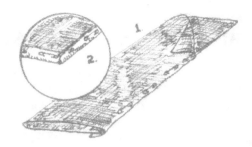

Use of blanket pins.

Our wire crews also walked. We alternated climbing poles for maybe 10 miles...then, if our tanks had won the battle, we would send one crew ahead and lay wire up to them for another six miles. It was a great job, by comparison. Even if we did walk up to 10 miles a day, it was usually less because we shared...and climbed only every other pole.

From our base in Apach, our combat commands took turns clearing out the small towns on our side of the Siegfried Line. The people on small farms here had kept to their homes. It was an area that may have sympathies with either France or Germany. Saw some women today. One waved from the window of her street-side home, where she washed dishes. Wash water ran out from below the window through a trough to the street. The other woman ignored us as she knelt by a stream scrubbing her clothes in a small stream-connected shed that looked like a boat house. We had a lengthy discussion about the merits of washing clothes at a spring house, then decided it was just protection from the cold. I could always count on an exchange of ideas when riding in the halftrack with Frank and Hap! The ride was deceptively safer when we could see people at their farmwork along the way.

Working out of Apach, we ran wire under shell-burst conditions up to Laumsfeld by November 16.

Our Combat Command ran up against the Siegfried Line for a few days. The closer we got to the Saar River the slower the going. By November 21st the town of Apach became a home base while our combat commands took turns attacking the small towns and pillboxes in between.

On the 21st of November we slept in a barn down the street from where we stayed last night. We only remain one night when a Frenchman offers hospitality, and ask only for barns. When it is our turn for a rotation to the rear of our division, we usually hole-up in the town two nights. Our 2 1/2-ton trucks make a trip to the supply depot; then the Command (A, B, or R) is off again, trying to burst through the well-fortified defenses.

By November 22, 1944, still in France, our jeep was starting to make gurgling noises, as though to celebrate the fall of Metz. That was the day Hoby and I drove back to a Maintenance Battalion, where he helped install a new motor. My job was to scrounge a better muffler for our vehicle. I found one on an otherwise wrecked jeep. We had to stay for a few days on account of parts, but were anxious to hit the road to be back with our outfit. On the 26th we headed forward again, with Hoby driving as fast as feasible with a new motor, to gain the protection of our division...before they disappeared across the Siegfried Line.

With Hoby driving, and no convoy to worry about, I paid more attention to the French

Dear Dad,   Somewhere near the front   NOV 16, 44
                                    PS NOV 19

Found this V-mail in the track & am just sending a short note to let you know every thing is running smoothly. No, I don't have that five dollars yet. Don't send it to me if you haven't already. We have been using Francs over here, even get paid in Francs (I mean with Francs). I'm writing this with gloves on, so pardon the irregularity. Tell Mother V-mail writing was good. I've had no trouble reading any. Explain to all the kin folks that if I don't get a chance to write X-mas cards its not 'cause I'm not thinking of them. I have X-mas V-mail (home made) in a dry place if **V ... — MAIL** I can get at it. Love

November 16: Note the censor's stamp. I can refresh my memory with letters written home and clippings about the 10th Armored. We aren't even supposed to mention the weather, but if the weather is the same all over, it doesn't matter. Where the date goes, at the top, was another place to communicate: "Somewhere on the ocean," "... near the front," or "at the front," "... in France," or "in Germany."

countryside on the way back. Bleak and battle-scarred, it was nevertheless still pictur-esque.

Particularly interesting were small roadside villages. Doorways, crowding the house next door, were graced with slight stone arches, echoing steps below made of solid stone; worn through the years to a cupped slope in the middle. Gray cobblestone streets wound between connected houses interspersed with flower boxes. Too high to be mud-splashed, they are dust-covered and dull with the bleakness of approaching Winter. The street itself looked like most of our 280 tanks had passed this way. In places, displaced cobblestones had been roiled up through the mud of deep ruts.

Coming through France, the rain seemed to follow us. Water pooled the ground in ruts and bomb craters, most muddy to obscure the depth of the hole, so Hoby tried to avoid them where possible. We splashed our way up to the Siegfried Line by way of Metz, crossing the Moselle River for the second time at Thionville.

Again, it was dark when we approached the bridge at Thionville. An ack-ack battery was on the alert for German planes, but all we heard was Washing Machine Charlie. Maybe the enemy was tired of trying to blow up the bridge. Our main thoughts were on taking the correct fork in the road. Our topic of conversation was whether or not we could get a hot meal when we got back.

While we were gone, our wire crews were kept busy laying wire to small towns North of Metz that fell into our lap after a certain amount of convincing. Even though the actual front was at the Siegfried Line we had to capture the small towns in our area and rid them of German troops.

We returned just as Combat Command "A" was attacking the fortifications, a string of small towns in valleys interlaced with pillboxes and connected with hills and streams. Our first day on the job we were assigned to the halftrack (ostensibly for protection) and ran a line up this little valley with cement fortifications on either side. There we waited, and waited for our infantry to advance, then had to come back the next day, and we had a command post to lay it to!

By December first, the Tenth was knocking at the gates of Merzig, although some pillboxes of the Siegfried Line stood in the way. Frontal assaults didn't work too well. Our tank guns weren't powerful enough. It was more effective when we brought up the 155 howitzers, using them like rifles. The shock stunned the enemy, making our infantry immune to any machine-gun fire until they lobbed a couple of grenades inside. The terrain proved much too rugged to continue these maneuvers, however, and beyond the hills lay the river and Merzig, on the other side. Our tanks did punch through, arriving at the bridge just in time to see it blown into the air...and water.

One of the problems with clearing out the pillboxes was that we needed to occupy them or the Nazis would filter back in at night and we would have to clear them out again, while losing some good men. Our tank infantry needed to support the tanks, not occupy pillboxes! We found that, in another sector, tank outfits had brought up bulldozers and covered the pillboxes with dirt, sometimes with a squad of defenders inside. That way they didn't have to worry about a percentage of infiltration! The most effective, and fastest way of eliminating the pillbox threat was to call in an air strike beforehand, which would bomb out the pillboxes and also knock out some "outside' machine guns and anti-aircraft guns where possible; then we could mop up, if the timing was perfect.

Another way we smashed through the Siegfried Line was to keep moving up the Division 105's and 155's, both to protect the infantry and to blast the pillboxes. A good description of this comes from the History of the 309th, a battalion using 155's in a sector to the North of us: "As the attack slowly smashed its way through the pillbox-studded Siegfried Line our Artillery had to move forward to keep within range. This was done in a leapfrog manner when 'C' Battery jumped 'A' and 'B' Batteries to set up in front of them in a position that was literally a sea of slushy snow and liquid mud. In this muddy ground it was practically impossible to keep the gun trails from jumping the pits. Each time the guns would smash back through the log-braced trail pits they would have to be winched out by the tractors and re-laid. During the night of the 4th, each of the guns had to be winched out and re-laid three times. It was a hellish night to put it mildly."

It was time to break through the famous Siegfried Line at another point. Instead, Command "B" headed toward Luxembourg. Our Command, "A," was awaiting reinforcements in Apach, having borne the recent brunt of fire from the pillboxes.

A fleet of 2 1/2 ton trucks is loaded ready to go. Drivers relax before taking to the twisting roads of France. Many trucks tow trailers, also chock-full with supplies for the front... part of the Red-Ball Express. The only thing that the 2 1/2 ton truck had over the halftrack was that we could sleep in it. However, since we were in combat we hadn't slept in a vehicle. When it was warmer we slept under our halftrack a couple of times for protection from the flak, but it wouldn't be much use if the enemy could get off a direct artillery shot against the side of our track, whether we were in it or under it. (Courtesy of U.S. Army Signal Corps.)

Combat Command "B" was rushed to Bastogne to help stem the Nazi Winter offensive...which turned out to be the enemy's last dying gasp, but which scared the bejabbers out of everybody. This action just prolonged the war during the Christmas Season of 1944. Our "A" and "R" commands followed to the Luxembourg area on the heels of "B" for about two weeks to keep pressure on the southern side of the bulge.

"A" followed soon after "B" in order to cover the bottom of the bulge and keep Hitler's Winter Offensive in a stream so it could be cut off. Since we were actually attached to Supreme Headquarters Allied Expeditionary Force it would have been difficult for Patton to wrest us away for any diversionary tactic, even if he wanted to. Patton really couldn't get permission for any intrusion into headquarters planning.

When our wireman, Frank Armbruster, connected into the Ninth Armored switchboard, he found a bonus; they were already tied into the 109th Infantry of the 28th Division. However, it was difficult to salvage much order out of the remainder of the 28th's Commands. They had taken the brunt of the Panzer attack and were thinned out considerably.

Just as our crews laid wire from Division Headquarters, in Mersch, up to our fighting outfits, we were subject to some incoming rounds, although the infantry holding the line took most of the shelling. Supposedly, we were there to hold the southern shoulder of the bulge and put some pressure on the advancing Germans. At that time we weren't sure whether or not we would be making the breakthrough, but it turned out the 4th Armored got the job. They had a full division, which, it turned out, was sorely needed.

Patton sent another division, the 26th Infantry, to follow the 4th Armored in large trucks. George Williams, a sergeant in Co. "M" heavy weapons platoon with the 26th Division relates an episode that shows Patton's adherence to flank protection when it was necessary. Patton pulled his 26th division out of the Metz area, where they were picking up replacements, and sent them up to the Bulge where they arrived Christmas night! Only a few days had elapsed since the 4th Armored drove up to Bastogne, but the 26th and the 80th were in back of them if they had been needed!

"We were outside Wiltz," said Williams, "and had set up a water-cooled 30, when we heard German voices in the dark. We spotted them and had our machine gun trained on them, when they must have heard something and sent up a flare. There we were, in full view, but our gunner let them have it at that time. He was shot, but they were stacked up like cordwood, laying on top of each other. I noticed the rest of the company had not come up as far as we had, so it was necessary to grab the machine gun and fall back without our assistant gunner, who had disappeared...probably into a nearby house, where the Germans were headed. I called in artillery on the vicinity of the house to protect him if he was still alive.

"The request somehow got routed through Corps Headquarters, and we got the benefit of a large number of back-up artillery. Just about that time, some Germans were searching the house, where our wounded gunner had dived under a bed. He was shooting at them with his 45 when the shells started to hit and they just up and left. Outside, after the barrage, one German remained in a nearby ditch, not wounded, but frozen to his position. Our assistant gunner, who had been bandaged by the civilians in the basement, captured him and took him back for questioning.

"The prisoner made a strange request," continued Williams. "He asked to be shown our belt-fed artillery, to confirm a rumor he had heard." Of course we had nothing like that - maybe later!

After Combat Command "A" had been at Mersch a couple of days, our crews realized

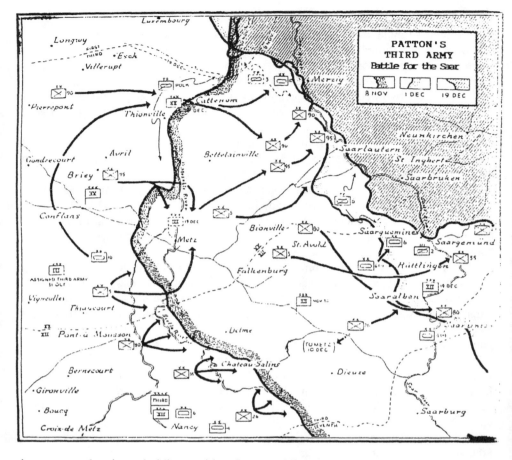

it was more than just a holding position. It seemed like the Germans knew we were there. They sent mail our way so we were always out shooting trouble on the lines. We kept the bulge from dipping South to cut off the Fourth Armored, which was having a hard enough time rushing up to relieve Bastogne. They had to stop and re-group a couple of times, but finally made it by December 26...after a Christmas that was the least celebrated by the men of Bastogne as any in their memories, but they were thankful that they were alive.

The Germans found out that we were on their southern flank, and they must have just discovered that we were also in Bastogne. They knew our Combat Command "B" had lost some tanks, but they may not have known our supply lines were so much better than theirs that we could move out right away - as soon as our combat commands could get together again.

Even though we had an extremely long supply line it was well organized, with many ten-ton trucks that came to be known as the Red Ball Express. Augmented by the 2 1/2-ton trucks assigned to our divisions, the supply lines were always kept open. When a 2 1/2-ton truck would be lost or damaged, there was usually another to take its place. Stockpiles built up in England were still shuttling trucks to the front lines, and our Ordnance Battalions were repairing damaged ones.

On several occasions in their reports, our company officers had requested an additional truck or two in order to drive back and pick up wire from the supply depot. So far there were no "extra" trucks available.

The longer our supply lines became, the more trouble we had. Eventually, our company traded three 2 1/2-ton trucks for three halftracks. It was safer to drive a halftrack back for wire, easier to get along in the snow, and a lot better vehicle from which to lay wire. It could carry about nine miles of wire, and we liked the idea of steel sides instead of canvas ones! The halftrack was usually sent to the forward position to work back, while Hoby and I, with the jeep, worked forward.

We learned that with Patton's armor there was very little time to dig foxholes. In his speech to the Third Army before moving to the continent from England, he said: "There is no such thing as a foxhole war anymore. My men don't dig foxholes. I don't want them to. Foxholes only slow up the offensive. Keep moving! Don't give the enemy a chance to dig one. We'll win this war, but we'll win it only by fighting and showing the Germans we've got more guts than they have!"

Our attack position on December 19 was essentially a hold position for those divisions left on the Siegried Line front. The Tenth Armored shot up to Belgium. We had started to establish our reputation as one of Patton's fast-moving divisions. You may notice from the Third Army map that we had swept up from our "rest" area to pound on the Siegfried Line, then suddenly our CCB jumped all the way to Bastogne, with CCA going almost all the way.

When we returned to almost the same location and battered our way through the Siegfried Line it must have been a surprise to the German Command. They were beginning to have trouble figuring out where we were.

Patton was right! This type of dugout might be O.K. for infantry on a stabilized front, but armor should not stop long enough to prepare something like this. A few branches are better for camouflage because they are quicker. Early on soldiers were issued leggings, which did not protect us from water. It was faster to tuck pants into our boots. (Courtesy of U.S. Army Signal Corps.)

CHAPTER 6
BATTLE OF BASTOGNE

On December 16, 1944, Hitler set in motion the last forceful counterattack of World War II. He was so imbued with what he had created that he felt invincible, and he followed a pattern of not listening to his generals. They could see that this latest push was just serving up German soldiers on the altar of Hitler's ego.

Our generals thought it was Germany's last hurrah. Above all, Patton knew it. Eisenhower asked him how soon he could move his troops up there - Patton answered "Now." He knew we could do it! Patton's Headquarters knew something was about to break, and he had set up plans to cope with it with only a phone call!Combat Command "B" of the Tenth Armored was dispatched immediately. "A" and "R" had just come out of the line and weren't quite ready to go. I was in "A." I know one-third of our division made it to Bastogne in 48 hrs. as promised.

When they arrived, forward areas were in turmoil. Small bands of soldiers from broken units were standing off tanks with bazookas. Others were retreating. At the suggestion of Maj. General Troy Middleton of VIII Corps, Colonel Roberts had split his 10th Armored Command into three forces: (Lt. Col.) O'Hara, (Lt. Col.) Cherry, and (Maj.) Desobry, each to defend an important road leading into Bastogne.

Sergeant Frank Houston, of our Third Tank Battalion, happened to be with our Combat Command "B" at the opportune time. What makes it opportune is that he came back alive, after helping to stand off the attacking armies in this epic struggle. "When we arrived in Bastogne," he related, "we were separated into three task forces.

"Each of our forces was sent to block a road coming into town. Our team of about 30 tanks, complete with infantry, was called Cherry - that was our colonel's name. We had a tough assignment because we ran into elements of a Panzer division at Longvilly just as we had become bogged down in the mud with retreating vehicles blocking our way. Our movements were restricted so we had trouble getting off the first shots.

"Our mortar platoon was getting ready for support fire when they were over-run by German infantry attacking with the tanks. The Panzers caught us in the mud, but some of our tanks made it back to Bastogne and we were glad to be able to dish it out for a change.

"Actually, we just about made it back to Bastogne because we had to cut through part of another German division to make it. I think we surprised them before they could do anything about our small band of remaining tanks. Outside of town we took up positions behind a hill or in a depression where we could get off the first shot. Other tanks would come out from town to help with flanking actions. No matter what they threw at us we could hold."

The effort of these three forces bought some time until the 101st could be trucked in with their experienced bazooka teams. They arrived in time, driving all night with their lights on. Our forces had held up the Nazis for 36 hrs.

General McAuliffe arrived soon after his 101st troops to take charge of the defense of the town. Tank defense was left up to Colonel Roberts, who lined up our vehicles alongside buildings in the center of town, facing in opposite directions. They could be called on to defend an attack from any quarter! What infantry we had left would have to go out with the tanks to protect our tanks from German infantry with bazookas, or panderfausts.

The Tenth Armored tanks were down to two teams, but we were reinforced by more than a dozen tanks from the Ninth Armored, plus some from the 741st, a tank battalion that had pulled back from defense of twin towns of Krinkelt/Rocherath.

December 18: Our Combat Command "B" in Bastogne was told to maintain one radio channel with the 10th Armored at all times, preferably in the Recon net. Permission was granted for them to drop out of Command and Administration nets. On December 19 we were in touch with the 9th Armored Division by radio. Although not mentioned in General McAuliffe's letter to his troops, the 9th Armored had also rushed part of their division to Bastogne in time to help in defense of the town, and were practically chased there by a panzer division. Tenth Armored units had arrived within 48 hours, as promised.

I think Combat Command "B" of the 9th Armored was mistaken for our Combat Command "B" of the 10th Armored, whose colonel was running the tank protection part of the town defense. This may have contributed to lack of recognition of the Ninth's contribution. Without their 15 tanks we would have surely been in more trouble than we were in already, with seven Nazi divisions pushing to get through the critical intersection that we held. They could have gone around and kept going on the newly frozen ground of Winter but not without leaving their supply lines in jeopardy!

In spite of the heavy artillery barrage, communications had worked out very well. Our wire crew ran lots of wire to all perimeter observation stations, then kept it open to the switchboard by constantly shooting trouble with our jeep. The wire halftrack, with its 50-caliber machine gun, had been knocked out by an incendiary shell just outside our building.

By then we were almost surrounded, and attacks were starting to come from all directions. On the morning of the 19th, large trucks loomed out of the fog at one of our outpost villages just before all roads were closed off. It was the 101st Airborne Division coming, (almost) out of the clouds. They kept coming, truck after truck, packed to a total of over ten thousand stout-hearted men. The 101st came toward Bastogne, while other single units, separated from their divisions, either stayed to help or scrambled to get away.

Lt. John Hemcher, who had three tanks knocked out from under him in previous battles, recounted his experience in Bastogne: "We carried 97 rounds of 75 millimeter shells. Outside the tank we stored five or six 5-gallon cans of gas, which burned once in Bastogne from an artillery hit; but we put out the fire with an extinguisher carried in the tank. We used a camouflage net until a couple of hits burned it up, then we used tree branches. We would park our tank next to a building on the outskirts of Bastogne where we could hit the enemy when they attacked in our sector. We were shelled by artillery several times in Bastogne. Each time we would move the tank to a new location under cover of darkness, so we would be ready for the next day's attack. My tank, the 'Paoli Local,' helped in actual counter-attacks, as other tanks rolled out to join in the battle."

For artillery we had our 105's, some 105's from other cut-up outfits, and several 155's. With this amount of artillery, small villages outside of Bastogne were well within the range to be defended without moving the guns. Our three forces had moved back from Noville, Longvilly and Bras to three towns nearer Bastogne, while slowing up the overwhelming forces. This was quite a feat because an enemy Tiger tank could withstand direct hits against its heavily-armored slanted front.

For our tankers, it was a question of how best to knock out the tiger tanks, not whether or not it could be done. In talking about tank armament, Sgt. Houston disclosed: "Our 76's were much better than our 75's because of the longer barrels and higher velocity. With the 76's we could penetrate up to a Panther V but not a Tiger VI from the front."

It was a matter of out-flanking the Tiger tanks with our Shermans. We could move 26 miles per hour to their 8 m.p.h., while being able to move our turret on target automatically. The Tiger tanks had a hand-traversing mechanism that was slow, and the handle was overhead in an awkward position.

Hugh Rafferty, Medic with the 101st, tells about the epic trip his division made in the dead of night to reach Bastogne. Some of them were on passes so when they got back it was time to ship out, but hardly enough time to get their gear together. The following description is from Hugh's letters "to Mom."

"I got my pass to Paris around the fifteenth of Dec. and got back on the 17th, a Sunday night. The next morning when we got up we were told that we were restricted, but no one knew why. At eight o'clock that morning we got orders to be packed ready to move by two o'clock that afternoon.

"What a job. Every one had a mess of Christmas packages that they hadn't opened and I had a load of perfume I had brought back from Paris with me. So between running around looking for something to pack the perfume in, eating my Christmas packages and trying to get all my stuff together for packing, I was one busy boy. I finally got everything jammed into my duffel bag and stored away, but what a job it was of packing. I fairly forced my clothes into that bag.

"The worst part of this move was that we hadn't received any replacements for the fellows we lost in Holland and our equipment wasn't up to standard.

"Before we left Mourmelon our information was that we were going into Corp Reserve in case we were needed. What an understatement that was!

"After we got everything packed and stored, one way or another, we sat around until seven o'clock that night waiting for trucks. And what trucks! They were ten-ton tractor-trailer affairs with no tops. We were crowded in like sheep.

"The entire trip into Bastogne, or I should say the vicinity of Bastogne, was made at night. We left Mourmelon about 7 PM and got off the trucks about 10 AM the next morning and it was a cold, uncomfortable ride.

"Toward the last our trucks went very slow, stopping every few hundred yards. It was during these stops that we talked to fellows from several divisions who didn't know where their outfit was or what the score was. In fact, along our entire trip we met vehicles from all kinds of outfits coming away but we seemed to be the only ones going up.

"We got off the trucks in a little village outside of Bastogne. There were a few G.I.'s there, most of them lost. They claimed the Germans were all around and it turned out that they were, but we didn't believe it at the time.

"After spending one night in this village, we moved into Bastogne the next night. We moved through the city to the outskirts. Everyone slept for the rest of the night and when we woke the next morning we learned the road we had come in on was cut and we were surrounded. That was good news since we had left Mourmelon under strength and with equipment way below par. To be quite honest with you we expected to be captured and everyone began to get rid of all their German pistols, etc.

"The next day the attacks started all around us in an attempt to find a weak spot in our lines and they sure raised a lot of hell. One night I was in the aid station and a small force broke thru and raised all kinds of commotion. We were set up in a little village on the outskirts of Bastogne and a German tank came down the street firing point blank at every building. I'm telling you it isn't a pleasant sensation to look out the window and see a German tank sitting outside. We finally got the place cleared out but it was one noisy night. I could just see myself inside a P.O.W. camp looking out.

"Three days before Christmas we moved into a group of barracks in an old French army camp in Bastogne and set up a hospital to take care of the casualties that were piling up. We took over a large two story barn and used that for a hospital. Beds were merely straw on the floor and the wounded were laid shoulder-to-shoulder to conserve space.

"Christmas Eve the bombing started. It was about eight o'clock and I was at mass which was being held in another barracks. Just at the sermon the planes came over and began unloading. At first we thought it was artillery, but when they began landing in camp there wasn't any more doubt in our minds.

"We all cleared out of the building into what seemed to be a spotlight. The night was clear with a bright moon and together with the flares that the planes had dropped it seemed bright as day. I felt simply naked running across that white snow in such light.

"I got back to the hospital and of course there was a million and one things doing. The bombing lasted about a half hour although it seemed like a lifetime. The rest of the night was spent trying to get the patients quiet and to sleep. It is no easy task trying to convince someone that there is nothing to worry about when there is. After most of the patients had been quieted down, which was about 3 A.M., the planes came over again so it started all over again. It was during this second bombing that our Catholic Chaplain was killed. One of the things I have to do when I get home is to visit his mother in Washington. So Christmas was far from a holiday and I'm afraid the peace on earth good will toward men was far from present.

"The bombing continued every night with a couple exceptions, and when the planes came over before midnight it was certain they would be back at least once and often twice before morning. So it wasn't too pleasant a night for anyone.

"I was working nights, or I should say day and night. I would go to sleep there in the hospital about 7 A.M. and whenever I woke up, which was usually about two or three in the afternoon, I went back at it. After the first couple of days we had over 700 patients, and with such a few to take care of them as soon as one got up he went to work. We had all types of wounded from amputations to combat exhaustion, so it was no simple matter taking care of them.

"There were rumors flying around about the column pushing in to meet us for several days before it actually happened. I don't remember just what day it was that this column broke thru but I remember the relief it was to get the wounded evacuated back to where they could get better care. We checked out over 900 patients that morning, not counting the ones who had died. There were only about twenty of us running the so-called hospital, so you can get some idea of what kind of a job it was.

"After the siege had been lifted we moved out of Bastogne to a little village. It was some time after the first of the year that we found ourselves in trouble again. Apparently the Kraut was peeved about our getting away from him for he launched another big attack which had things in an uproar for a few hours. The attack was spearheaded by tanks and they over-ran the defense line and played merry hell in the rear. The infantry didn't follow their tanks close enough, so after the tanks had gone thru the fellows just stayed in their holes and knocked off the infantry as it came up. With no infantry support the tanks had to withdraw and when they came back quite a number were knocked out.

"This wasn't so easy as it sounds, though. When the tanks came thru they didn't save any shells. In the position they were in it was a simple matter to fire down into a foxhole and the fellows in those holes didn't have any need for medical attention. It wasn't a pretty sight, I assure you. This little battle went on for about four hours of almost hand-to-hand fighting before we had cleared things up.

"It took six hours of steady work fixing up the wounded and getting them evacuated.

It was after this that two companies were combined and were still half the strength of one original company. To say we were in a bad way would have been putting it mildly.

"Shortly after this we moved back into Bastogne which was fairly quiet and that is when we set up housekeeping in an apartment building. About a week later we were officially relieved and moved back about five miles."

That week Hugh was writing about was a week of chaos. Our men couldn't have held the town without the soldiers of the 101st because they were needed to fight alongside our tanks whenever the enemy put an organized attack against the town. There were many attacks that were repulsed. For an entire week the fighting was done without benefit of our air force. This was but one town in the important Battle of the Bulge, but it sat astride a multiple crossroads, and we held it.

Lineman Bob Anderson from the 150th Armored Signal Company was trouble shooting at a small town held by one of our tank units, shortly after the airborne troops had arrived. Bob had found the break in the line, checked in on his field phone, and was on his way back to Bastogne when he passed a double line of infantry on their way up to reinforce the town. It was a company from the 101st. "Some of them only wore wool knit hats, and they kept asking for spare helmets and K-rations," Bob related. "They acted like experienced troops who just knew what they needed."

We found out that these fellows weren't afraid of tanks or infantry, and carried bazookas and mortars to prove it. Their help was just what was needed to stand off the tank and infantry thrusts during the days to come. When an attack would be about to overcome our outposts they would charge out with our defending tanks. The enemy would leave behind smoking tanks and piles of their troops.

The men of our wire crew attached to CCB were kept busy shooting trouble on the lines, and replacing some of the wire. "After a couple of days we ran out of wire," according to Bob Anderson, of the 150th. "I was directed to take a driver in a 3/4 ton vehicle and go back to a supply depot at a small town outside Bastogne. I was to pick up whatever rolls of wire I could get on the truck. We arrived in the afternoon without incident. When about ready to go, I called back to Bastogne for information and was told in less than calm tones that the Germans were about to "time on target" the town. There was some vague statement about being almost surrounded and I was to get my ass back up there with wire!

"The driver and I started out. What I remember is that we were going against the traffic. Tanks and infantry seemed to be going up toward a battle; we were going back to Bastogne. We arrived in town and all was deadly quiet. No movement, no activity. We got to the hotel, and then all hell broke loose with the bombardment. A bit later that night we heard that the town was surrounded.

"By not really knowing the extent of the German strangle hold on the town, those of us on the 'bottom' just did what we had to do without concern for the next day. We worked one day, one hour at a time. Sleep was sporadic. I was working on the line near the top of a concrete pole at the edge of town where I could look out over some fields. The peaceful scene was interrupted with a mortar bombardment, with shells landing close to my position. It suddenly dawned on me...they are shooting at me. Apparently the mortars were positioned in the trees on the far side of the fields I had been observing. I 'burned' that pole on the way down. One doesn't exactly slide down a concrete telephone pole, but I did come down in a hurry. There was no point in giving the enemy a highly visible target. I took shelter in a building where some troops were holed up. A little later, when things calmed down, I went about my business and fixed the broken line.

General McAuliffe arrived soon after his 101st troops to take charge of the defense of the town. Tank defense was left up to Colonel Roberts, who lined up our vehicles alongside buildings in the center of town, facing in opposite directions. They could be called on to defend an attack from any quarter!

Headquarters of 10th Armored's CCB was a block away from the 101st Headquarters. Our switchboard was set up in the basement of a non-descript-looking building. The enemy couldn't see where we were, but their artillery seemed to find us, anyway. Our wire crew was kept busy finding breaks in the lines we ran to all positions.

December 20th unfolded with (comparatively) fresh 101st Airborne troops in place in the outskirts. We also had elements from several units, including the 705th Tank Destroyer Battalion, and various light tanks chased into town by Panzers. There the German tanks would meet the full force of our defense! The perimeter of town in all directions looked like a graveyard of German tanks of all sizes. We lost a lot of tanks, too, but the amount of firepower we were able to exert swayed each battle in our favor. However, we were running low on ammunition. Word had gone out to conserve ammunition. Tankers obtained some shells from knocked-out tanks that hadn't burned. Our tankers could salvage shells if a tank track had been damaged and any resulting fire had been put out.

Breakthroughs were tried on all sides of town. The medics had their hands full, and were glad for the medical supplies dropped during the brief interval of clear sky. Tanks had a way to help rescue a wounded infantryman. "We would come close so he could get into the escape hatch under the tank," said Lt. Hemcher, "They seldom knew that we had an escape hatch below the tank, and would try to crawl away from the tank, thinking we didn't see them. It was bad enough that they were shot. They didn't want to be crushed, as well. Then one of our men would lean out of the hatch and yell at the wounded man over the noise of machine gun fire and bursting shells. Often we had to crawl out and help the wounded man back to our tank."

Our switchboard operator had a little more security in the basement of a building, but he tended the switchboard with a carbine across his knees. Artillery bursts in the street and on the rooftops couldn't get at him, but during the interval of clear skies German planes bombed Bastogne and he heard one coming down through the roof and then each floor, landing in the room next to his. It was a dud! He said "I didn't have to go to the latrine after that because I already went."

The following account is from the History of the 741st Tank Battalion, an independent tank outfit that had been with Pennsylvania's 28th Division, including their parade together through the streets of Paris. They had moved into the outskirts of Bastogne from the North. There they stayed to pay back the enemy for tanks they had lost during the previous two days. Although they stayed in the North section of Bastogne, that didn't mean they remained in one position. They had to move their tanks almost daily to avoid artillery.

"In the ensuing weeks the 741st was tested under most severe battle conditions. Everyone was committed to the fighting; the cooks took up positions right along with the tank crewmen. The mechanics, supply personnel and company clerks all engaged the enemy one way or another. Acts of heroism were conducted by so many that it would be inappropriate to mention any names. As a group, the 741st fought with valor side by side with the infantry and held the North corner. The Germans did not go through us and everyone should be justly proud. Many stories are passed around about this action at the reunion; most of them are true."

German Tiger tanks were our most menacing prey...but at Bastogne we were their prey as they surrounded us like wolves. Our tankers couldn't use evasive tactics, but they did have a littered battlefield so they could hide behind knocked-out Tiger tanks and slug it out - our 76's against their 88's. To swing the battle in our favor we had lots of bazookas, manned mainly by the 101st. They hit the enemy tanks from the side and mowed down Kraut infantry using M1 rifles, B.A.R.'s, light and heavy mortars, 30-caliber and 50-caliber machine guns and hand grenades. Some German tanks were knocked out with 105 and 155 howitzers.

The Germans were losing so many men they came up with a surrender ultimatum on December 22. This elicited the famous reply by Brig. Gen. McAuliffe, as described in this letter to his troops:

HEADQUARTERS 101st AIRBORNE DIVISION
Office of the Division Commander
24 December, 1944
To the Men of the 101st:(Referring to Merry Christmas)

What's Merry about all This, you ask? We're fighting - it's cold - we aren't home. All true but what has the proud Eagle Division accomplished with its worthy comrades of the 10th Armored Division, the 705th Tank Destroyer Battalion and all the rest?

Just this: We have stopped everything that has been thrown at us from the North, East, South and West. We have identifications from four German Panzer Divisions, two German Infantry Divisions, and one German Parachute Division. These units, spearheading the last desperate German lunge, were headed straight West for key points when the Eagle Division was hurriedly ordered to stem the advance. How effectively this was done will be written in history; not alone in our Division's glorious history but in World history.

The Germans actually did surround us; their radios blared our doom. Their commander demanded our surrender in the following impudent arrogance.

"To the U.S.A. Commander of the encircled town of Bastogne:

The fortune of war is changing. This time the U.S.A. forces in and near Bastogne have been encircled by strong German armored units.

More German armored units have crossed the river Ourthe near Ortheuville, have taken Marche and reached St. Hubert by passing through Hombres-Silbert-Tillet. Libramont is in German hands.

There is only one possibility to save the encircled U.S.A. troops from total annihilation: that is the honorable surrender of the encircled town. In order to think it over a term of two hours will be granted beginning with the presentation of this note.

If the proposal should be rejected one German Artillery Corps and six heavy A-A Battalions are ready to annihilate the U.S.A. troops in and around Bastogne. The order for firing will be given immediately after this two hour's term.

All the serious civilian losses caused by this artillery fire would not correspond with the well known American humanity.

The German Commander"

The German Commander received the following reply:
22 December 1944
"To the German Commander:
N U T S !
The American Commander"

Allied Troops are counterattacking in force. We continue to hold Bastogne. By holding Bastogne we assure the success of the Allied Armies.

General Patton's Prayer

Nous publions ci-dessous dans son texte original, la savoureuse prière du Général G. Patton Jr. publiée lors de l'offensive d'hiver allemande en 1944—1945. Cette prière avait été formulée par le grand général dans la chapelle de la „Fondation Pescatore" à Luxembourg quelques jours avant Noël 1944.

„Le Drapeau"

«Sir, this is Patton talking. The last fourteen days have been straight hell. Rain, snow, more rain, more snow — and I'm beginning to wonder what's going on at Your headquarters. Whose side are You on, anyway?

«For three years my chaplains have been explaining this as a religious war. This, they tell me, is the Crusades all over again, except that we're riding tanks instead of chargers. They insist we are here to annihilate the German Army and the godles Hitler so that religious freedom may return to Europe.

«Up until now I have gone along with them, for You have given us Your unreserved cooperation. Clear skies and a calm sea in Africa made the landings highly successful and helped us to eliminate Rommel. Sicily was comparatively easy, and You supplied excellent weather for our armored dash across France, the greatest military victory that You have thus far allowed me. You have often given me excellent guidance in difficult command decisions and You have led German units into traps that made their elimination fairly simple.

«But now, You've changed horses in midstream. You seem to have given Von Rundstedt every break in the book and, frankly, he's been beating hell out of us. My army is neither trained nor equipped for winter warfare. And, as You know, this weather is more suitable for Eskimos than for southern cavalrymen.

«But now, Sir, I can't help but feel that I have offended You in some way. That suddenly You have lost all sympathy with our cause. That You are throwing in with von Rundstedt and his paperhanging god. You know without me telling You that our situation is desperate. Sure, I can tell my staff that everything is going according to plan, but there's no use telling You that my 101st Airborne is holding out against tremendous odds in Bastogne, and that this continual storm is making it impossible to supply them even from the air. I've send Hugh Gaffey, one of my ablest generals, with his 4th Armored Division, north toward that all-important road center to relieve the encircled garrison, and he's finding Your weather much more difficult than he is the Krauts.

«I don't like to complain unreasonably, but my soldiers from the Meuse to Echternach are suffering the tortures of the damned. Today I visited several hospitals, all full of frostbite cases, and the wounded are dying in the fields because they cannot be brought back for medical care.

«But this isn't the worst of the situation. Lack of visibility, continued rains, have completely grounded my air force. My technique of battle calls for close-in fighter-bomber support, and if my planes can't fly, how can I use them as aerial artillery? Not only is this a deplorable situation, but, worse yet, my reconnaissance planes haven't been in the air for fourteen days, and I haven't the faintest idea of what's going on behind the German lines.

«Dammit, Sir, I can't fight a shadow. Without Your cooperation from a weather standpoint, I am deprived of an accurate disposition of the German armies, and how in hell can I be intelligent in my attack? All this probably sounds unreasonable to You, but I have lost all patience with Your chaplains who insist that this a typical Ardennes winter, and that I must have faith.

«Faith and patience be damned! You have just got to make up Your mind whose side You're on. You must come to my assistance, so that I may dispatch the entire German Army as a birthday present to Your Prince of Peace.

«Sir, I have never been an unreasonable man. I am not going to ask You for the impossible. I do not even insist upon a miracle, for all I request is four days of clear weather.

«Give me four clear days so that my planes can fly; so that my fighter-bombers can bomb and strafe, so that my reconnaissance may pick out targets for my magnificent artillery. Give me four days of sunshine to dry this blasted mud, so that my tanks may roll, so that ammunition and rations may be taken to my hungry, ill-equipped infantry. I need these four days to send von Rundstedt and his godless army to their Valhalla. I am sick of this unnecessary butchery of American youth, and in exchange for four days of fighting weather, I will deliver You enough Krauts to keep Your bookkeepers months behind in their work.

«Amen.»

We know that our Division Commander, General Taylor will say: "Well Done!"

We are giving our country and our loved ones at home a worthy Christmas present and by being privileged to take part in this gallant feat of arms are truly making for ourselves a Merry Christmas.

(signed)
McAuliffe
Commanding

Patton's headquarters was located nearby, at Luxembourg. Jim Clark, sergeant in charge of switchboards at Third Army Headquarters, thought highly of General Patton, and is proud to have served under him. "It was a requirement of Patton's that we sweep out the headquarters location, and keep it clean. This meant no mud tracked in at any time! Often we arrived late in the evening, swept out the broken glass and litter from a battle after cleaning our boots," related Sergeant Clark. "But Patton was very fair, and I think he made fewer mistakes than other generals who had similar responsibilities, especially in battle.

"Around 10:30 one night General Patton said: 'I want to talk to Lucky Tac.' [Tactical planning officers at their location.] At that time Third Army did not have a line to Lucky Tac. After checking quickly to make sure, I called the general back, identified myself, and said, 'General, we do not have a line to Lucky Tac.' This probably took longer than he was accustomed to waiting. Nevertheless, Patton calmly apologized, saying, 'I'm sorry, sergeant, I meant Lucky Rear.'"

Asked what impressed him the most during the Battle of the Bulge, from a viewpoint at Third Army Headquarters, Clark answered, "The American soldier could assess the situation, improvise, and take immediate action. We found that the German officers could do this, but their enlisted men could not. This proved true especially in the Battle of the Bulge, according to many reports that we received."

The frustration of General Patton was concealed from his men, because he was always a hard taskmaster. This in no way diminished their respect for him as they continued to be cooped up together at the Foundation Pescatore, a home for older ladies at Luxembourg. Patton was mainly frustrated by something he couldn't do anything about, the weather. He finally disclosed this frustration in the prayer on the preceeding page, printed in Le Drapeau.

Another prayer was published for all Third Army personnel. This one was more official and was included with General Patton's Christmas Greetings:

Almighty and merciful Father, we humbly beseech Thee, of Thy great goodness, to restrain these immoderate rains with which we have to contend. Grant us fair weather for battle. Graciously hearken to us as soldiers who call upon Thee that, armed with Thy power, we may advance from victory to victory, and crush the oppression and wickedness of our enemies, and establish Thy justice among men and nations.

Amen.

On the reverse side was printed Patton's Christmas Greeting:

To each officer and soldier in the Third United States Army, I wish a Merry Christmas. I have full confidence in your courage, devotion to duty, and skill in battle. We march in our might to complete victory. May God's blessing rest upon each of you on this Christmas Day.

(signed)
G. S. Patton, Jr.
Lieutenant General Commanding, Third United States Army

This prayer was sent to the troops on December 22nd, the same day that General Patton made his more raucous prayer. Think what you will; the next day the weather cleared! A lot is written about what happened when the weather cleared, but it all seems anti-climatic. Now we knew we could hold out.

Patton pulled out all the stops to win, and he wanted to be blessed, because, like the rest of us, he believed we were in the right!

After the surrender offer was scoffed at, the defenders were hit with even larger concentrations of large enemy guns and had to contend with the indomitable 88's mounted on tanks and 88 field guns dug in just beyond the town outskirts. It must have been tough on the Germans, losing so many men. It was tough enough on our troops.

Blistering attacks were fought off for days under an overcast sky. Then a light snow began to fall. For a while, it looked like our air force was going to be kept out of the battle. The skies finally cleared enough for planes to drop ammunition and food, but not enough to call for bomber strikes against the enemy.

Shortly after Patton's prayer, gliders were able to bring coveted gasoline to Bastogne. It was December 23rd. One glider contained a team of surgeons to help care for the several hundred wounded in the make-shift hospital. Help was on the way, but not before the Luttwaffe passed overhead with a couple of bombing runs, thereby losing some more of their planes. Weather improved daily, and many glider runs were made, and colored parachutes were dropped with supplies.

Information on battle progress was being relayed by radio to Tenth Armored Headquarters, which had moved up to Mersch from Luxembourg with our other two combat commands. We had our hands full just North of there at Echternach, where Combat Command A and R were preventing the surrounding armies from expanding to the South.

Back at Mersch, the Tenth Armored's administration channel was jammed by the enemy on December 24, attesting to how well the Bastogne defenses were holding up. We had been having trouble all of December, with a strange station in our net, calling themselves CCX. They didn't know the password, and never learned it from listening in. Sometimes we could get a password over a line we had just laid...from someone who knew who was on the field phone.

Wire was usually more dependable than radio when officers wanted to communicate in private. This net intrusion was handled on Christmas Day, 1944. Our Tenth Armored Headquarters tried to help the situation with a request for Third Army Headquarters to make a triangulation with their special radio tracks. Our headquarters report for the day listed the request in this manner: "Radio: Requested Army to take direction finding reading on suspected enemy station in G-4(F) net. Station found to be CC X using wrong code sign. Other operations normal."

Another interesting report comes from our Signal Company Historical Record. It gives the Company Headquarters matter-of-fact point of view: "On the 29 December 1944, the division was moved from the Ardennes sector minus one combat command. The combat command remaining was at Bastogne, with the 101st Airborne Division, during its famous encirclement. Our equipment there consisted of a 399 radio, a wire halftrack and a quarter ton, 4 x 4, trouble shooting vehicle. The radio was remoted to the basement of the building and provided excellent communication. Wire crews put wire in and maintained it to all units in area as well as OP and road defense positions. As such it proved indispensable and was a very major item in the defense of Bastogne. Wire trouble shooters were continually repairing line breaks due to continuous artillery and air bombing.

"Casualties were one wire man killed and one severely wounded while maintaining wire in vicinity of switchboard. The wire halftrack was a complete loss as was the SCR 399, as the result of an incendiary bomb. The signal equipment was replaced immediately but other items required ten days to two weeks.

"Upon the completion of their task at Bastogne, the combat command again joined the division and was refitted for combat. Vehicular losses were, in general, heavy but vehicles with radios were not above the average losses."

Regardless of the Krauts' overwhelming numbers, by the end of the day more enemy bodies and tanks were piled up at the battle site, which changed day-by-day or hour-by hour 'til the town was ringed with burnt-out vehicles; mostly theirs. We welcomed each attack with open guns.

Tanks were so hot from firing that when there was a lull in the firing, or a let-up in the attack, tankers would heat C-rations on the tank. "Enemy infantry would attack at dusk, or after dark, using flares. After we fought them off would be a good time to heat C-rations while the tank was still hot," said Lt. Hemcher. He also spoke of having to use his sidearm on more than one occasion, the attackers came so close.

When hit, a tank would burn for two days. Gas cans stashed on the outside would burst and the tankers duffel, absorbing the gas, would burn like a torch, adding to the burning oil. Previously, Hemcher had tried to pull his buddy from a burning tank, but had to stop when ammunition burst around him.

We learned that Hitler's Ardennes offensive had been halted on Christmas Day by the Seventh Armored, and the 2nd Armored had completely defeated a Panzer division after a day-long tank battle. Patton's famous 4th Armored relieved Bastogne on December 26, adding to the ring of burned-out German vehicles on the southern side of Bastogne. They also lost a lot of tanks and had to re-group a couple of times before they could blast through.

Lothar H. Miller, whose job was to interrogate prisoners, spent Christmas Eve with some of his 10th Armored Buddies in Combat Command "B" headquarters in Hotel Lebrun in Bastogne. "It was snowing," relates Miller. "Softly, dark. Those sentimental G.I.'s remembered it was Christmas. Remembered; 'there ought to be a Christmas tree.' There always had been one at home, as far back as anyone could recall. A Christmas tree; hey there has to be ornaments. OK, so the G.I.'s scrounged; they were good at that. Tree cut from the surrounding country side - now, the ornaments. Cellars, attics, produced some tinsely things. Christmas Eve, softly snowing. The tree stood straight and green in the dimly lit headquarters - the lobby of Hotel Lebrun. Combat Command 'B,' 10th Armored Division, had its headquarters here, where that 'unlimited capabilities' smart ...lieutenant of IPW #112 had put them six long days ago. It was M/Sgt. Bean who found the tattered rag doll and hung it on the tree.

"The drone. Airplanes. How could they fly tonight? The crunch of the 500-pound bombs exploded across the town, but tonight? They should know it is Christmas Eve and snowing! The bomb crunch marched closer - eh, one landed very, very nearby in the street, sending its shrapnel through the lobby window. One screaming piece went right through the rag doll at abdomen level. Wounded. Perhaps dead.

"No, not dead, for in the dim dawn the Sgt. appeared and pinned a Purple Heart on the rag doll. Perhaps the doll would die, but not in SPIRIT."

Such was the spirit of Christmas. Like hordes of Huns the Germans tried to break our spirit, but failed. Our men had prevailed for one more night.

The Germans had so many divisions in the area, Bastogne was attacked once more, on January third and fourth. Once more their attack failed. By now they were having trouble escaping from a trap of their own making. If Montgomery had moved quickly to close the gap from the North, or if Patton had been sent a bit further we might have trapped them for sure. Probably Monty should have done the job...Patton could have done the job...but then, that would embarrass Monty, who had to be 100% sure it was a good tactical move before he committed his troops. General Montgomery really was a decisive person; it just took him longer to decide. With the decision made, he was good at following through...eventually!

Hitler's Winter Offensive of Forty Four was lost on the shoulders of General McAuliffe of the 101st Airbourne and Colonel Roberts of the 10th Armored at Bastogne. The stamina and invincibility of their men rested with what their leaders had instilled in their minds. One of these leaders was General Patton, who had devised the mode of operation of our armored divisions, whose rules told how to think. Patton was glad to pin a medal on McAuliffe, who was willing to share the credit for defending the town of Bastogne.

After a few more days the weather cleared and our planes took command of the sky - and the roads below. The panzer divisions were at the end of their fuse, where they sputtered to a halt.

Our Combat Command "A" was about to be sent back to a staging area near Metz. That may be why we aren't shown on page 62 the map...or it could be we were assigned to SHAEF for a couple of days, or we may have lost our identity when we used the Ninth Armored switchboard. Perhaps General Patton wanted to be sure our division was available to send to the Saar-Moselle triangle as soon as possible and would not be tied up by SHAEF Headquarters!

It had taken us over a month to contain the 13-division German prong, aimed at Antwerp as a blitzkrieg, but reduced to a dribble as a few of their troops escaped through our net. Hitler was crazy to start this attack, instead of trying to defend the Rhine, but sane enough to know the Russians were coming, and he tried to make us hunker down in a stalemate for the Winter. It didn't work. The French civilians, who all along had worked for victory, now had a taste of it and would not let go. They helped however they could.

Two linemen contemplate Wire Weasel damage beyond repair by artillery toward the end of the Bastogne conflict in early January.

Doughboys Stage Modern Alamo in Heroic Stand at Bastogne

Wreckage of 87 German Tanks Attest Deadly Fire of Defense

1 Supreme Headquarters Allied Expeditionary Force, Paris, Dec. 28 (AP)

2 If the Alamo had been reached in time; if fleet-guarded troopships could have gunned their way through to Bataan, that would have been the story of Bastogne, the American Arnheim, as it appeared today.

It was a bloody, heroic, suicide stand with promise of a bright ending.

The men who fought and died in the tank-pounded outposts around the town for a week, and some of them probably still are fighting and dying there, cannot yet be identified.

Tied Up Five German Divisions

3 They are several thousand strong—or were when the battle started in which they tied up the better part of five German divisions and denied Field Marshal von Rundin his offensive bulge.

But it can be disclosed that many were veterans of battles fought under much the same circumstances.

Neither can the armor and infantry which fought their way through to them be identified. In that drive the American tanks carried 10 miles or more up the Arlon-Bastogne Road and held the corridor open through the first 24-36 hours with a determination which suggested it would stay open.

2 During the week-long siege, the Bastogne pocket was under day and night pressure from every side against odds comparable to those which British parachute troops faced at Arnheim, in Holland. There was no way of telling how much longer the American garrison could have held out, but the stories of the men who fought there now make clear how they withstood the siege.

GI Joes of Bastogne are Hailed by British

London, Dec. 28 (AP) *The Evening News* today hailed the "GI Joes of Bastogne" as the equals of Britain's Red Devils of Arnheim and among the greatest heroes of the war.

"All America honored the men of Arnheim," said the editorial. "All Britain today honors the men of Bastogne."

4 "It was not for the men of Bastogne to ask, as the people at home have asked, why the High Command was taken unawares. It was their task to stand firm at the crossroads."

The garrison was bolstered during its siege by the biggest aerial supply task force ever attempted by the Allies, headquarters said today as a part of the story unfolded.

At least 342 C-47 transport and 50 glider drops were made in four days. These missions were carried out on December 23, 24, 26 and 27.

When the relief column burst through, it found the Americans not smashed back into the streets but clinging grimly to the outpost line.

There was no indication at headquarters that the Germans had been able to smash into the town itself from any side, although time and again tanks did break through the perimeter.

Around the shell-torn Bastogne ring the wreckage of 87 German tanks attested to what success the Nazi thrusts enjoyed.

Thus far there is no official word to indicate what the next developments may be. There are these possibilities:

5 The Battle-worn Bastogne defense force might be withdrawn as quickly as it is possible to move in fresh troops.

5 The whole force might be withdrawn through the corridor and Bastogne given up— its job done.

5 It might only be supplied and reinforced quickly as possible to continue the holdout in the event a Nazi counterattack pinches off the corridor.

---

1 *Interesting Official Summary*
2 *Credit given to British by comparison*
3 *Downplay of number of German divisions (Seven had been mentioned in Gen. McAuliffe's letter)*
4 *British "slight dig" aimed at American High Command*
5 *Tactical possibilities mentioned (No mention of cutting off enemy corridor)*

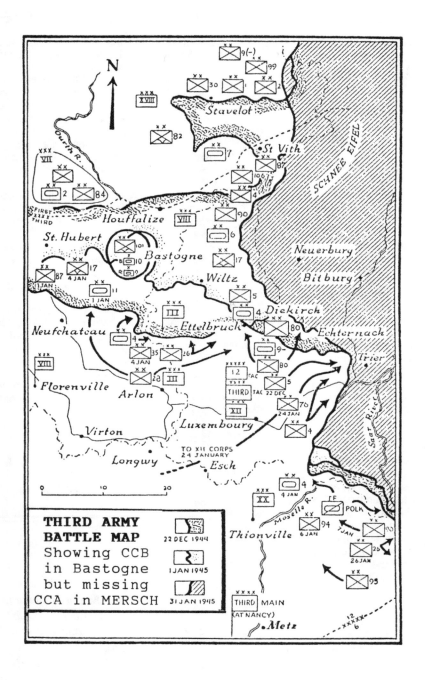

N

THIRD ARMY BATTLE MAP
Showing CCB in Bastogne but missing CCA in MERSCH

22 DEC 1944
1 JAN 1945
31 JAN 1945

The Battle of the Bulge eclipsed more than just the town of Bastogne. By the end of January, most units were back to their previous assignments...furthering the attack on Germany. Winter was upon us, and intermittent snows were falling on the European front.

We still had to get the wire through, one way or another. All wire crews were experiencing the same problems, and finding ingenious ways to solve them.

By January 31, 1945, thousands of white camouflage suits were being made by civilians at Hayange, France

This description, by James Cannon of the Stars and Stripes staff, was dated January 6, 1945:

Thin Line Holds Fast

"By the afternoon of the 18th, a task force of the Tenth was rolling into Bastogne. It is largely responsible for holding the city until the first element of the 101st Airborne Div. arrived on Dec. 19 to make one of the bravest stands in the history of men of war. From the time it went into action until the Fourth Armored Div. broke through the ring around the city the Tenth fought continually, driving into any section of the area where a fresh breakthrough threatened.

"In support of a battalion of the 101st and elements of the Ninth Armored Div., units of the Tenth figured in the destruction of a German counter-attack southwest of Bastogne. This action has been described as the fiercest battle of the Bastogne defense."

Attacked from Three Sides

"Col. L. Roberts of the Tenth, who directed the defense of Bastogne until the 101st arrived, dispatched units of his outfit north and east of the town to defend the approaches at Noville, Longvilly and Bras. With the 101st they held until Dec. 21, although attacked from three sides. Then they fell back to high ground. At Longvilly the tankers were cut off and surrounded, but shot their way out."

An example of Yankee versatility is this unusual photo by Sgt. W.F. Lovell of the 166th Photo Company. Signal Corps lineman use a line tightner while tapping in to existing wire in Koenigsmacher, France. One of them seems to be standing on air. (Courtesy of Patton Library.)

CHAPTER 7
THROUGH THE SIEGFRIED LINE

First to return from Bastogne was Staff Sergeant Andy Osborne and his driver in the battle-scarred jeep. Then came Henry Allbritton, Bob Anderson and John Cotter, switchboard operator. Harvey Otis had been killed and Sgt. Al Lynch seriously wounded when an 88 shell exploded on the street where they were shooting trouble on the lines. Harvey, who always wore his tie, was the perfect soldier.

Bob Anderson explained the trouble shooting precisely: "Now this task doesn't sound too difficult. Test and look, test and look, then splice. The problem we faced was that the job was accomplished under an almost continuous bombardment by German 88's. So there was a lot of duck and hide going on besides the test and look. Then there were several more obstacles facing the wireman. The first was the cold. The second was snow. The third was darkness. It seemed to me that we did a good part of our work on repair at night under blackout conditions. While it may not seem important, a major problem was keeping track of our gloves. One couldn't splice with gloves on, so it was necessary to stuff them in a pocket. If a glove was lost or misplaced it was impossible to get a new issue. Thus, one had to be extremely vigilant about the location of one's gloves."

While we were stationed in the Metz area, waiting for replacements, our main job was to pick up wire, because it was in short supply. Much had been laid after the battle for Metz was over, and was still in fair shape. Even radio operators were put to work at this job, to keep them busy. It was mainly a matter of finding out which wire might still be in use. Sometimes that was hard to do.

Bill Terza, of the 150th, was picking up wire with his crew of radio operators when he ran into a humorous situation. "We would ring three times," said Terza, "and then if there was no answer, we would pick up the wire. We would cut it to find an end, then roll it up. Suddenly, a sergeant from an anti-aircraft battery came up in his jeep, boiling mad: 'What's the matter with you! You cut off the wire to my only battery!' I explained that we were told to ring just three times. He said 'Gimmie that phone!' But it rang several times and he went off in a huff, muttering 'They must be asleep again.'"

About this time our division started a Radio School, which was operational 'til after the end of the war. Bill Terza, who was a staff sergeant at the time, tells how it came about: "Colonel Graham came to John Zdyrko and I, saying 'You know, we have lost a number of radio operators due to casualties, and I would like you to start a Radio School.' Starting with my half track and its two radios, we acquired a couple of 2 1/2-ton trucks, some extra radio equipment, and some keys. A lot of the radio equipment we had on hand because we would furnish needed supplies to divisions who were with us for flank protection. We acquired a couple of heavy-duty tank batteries. Almost before we had the school set up, 35 recruits arrived who had already been screened for code aptitude."

We thought we were rushed South to Metz to either start a new attack or rest up for a couple days and then advance. What we did was to operate out of Apach, France. From there the Tenth armored was put on an "as needed" alert. That meant a couple of days taking towns at the rate of five or more a day, then back to Apach again while we waited for C.C.B. to get re-outfitted.

During our in-between days I got a chance to go to a dance at Metz. There was this French girl who could dance up a storm, even while in a close embrace. For one evening there was no thought of wire, and I tried not to talk to her about splices and field phones.

Then an earlier acquaintance of hers came up and actually grabbed her away. Since he was drunk and also wearing a side-arm I elected not to play hero. Anyway, that was the last woman I talked to until the end of the war.

Looking back on this series of small campaigns I finally figured out that Patton was told to clean up the Saar-Moselle triangle before moving ahead. We were privileged to be participants. Using methods practiced under Patton in his Desert Training Center by the Second Armored, our officers led the way with tanks, backed up by artillery. Sometimes it was the other way around, like most generals. The upper echelon still fought the war the old fashioned way. Our recon tanks always made contact with the enemy. This was one of Patton's training musts!

That's why we took so many towns in a day. With our wire halftrack and jeep, our crew laid wire to two towns on a good day, and we knew the other two teams were doing the same. When the 2 1/2-ton truck was not being used to pick up supplies we would use it to help lay wire. That's a total of eight towns. The reason we could do this was that we were not advancing like a front, but were running amuck behind the lines.

The recon tanks of our 90th Cavalry Reconnaissance Squadron often took towns on their own, raking German outposts with machine gun fire as they swept thru town. At that point it was too late for the enemy to set up a more effective road block. I'm convinced that during this period we started to establish our reputation (with the Germans) as the Ghost Division.

In this feat alone, we were adhering to Patton's idea of the correct use of armor. He had programmed our American armored divisions to operate with an entirely new method. Yes, it was a little risky, but saved a lot more lives than Montgomery's huge extravaganzas. For instance, Monty took such a long time getting ready to push South toward Bastogne after the Fourth Armored had broken through, it allowed many experienced Nazis to crawl

Wireman, somewhere near a river, December 1944.

Above left: In the 1st Army, linemen string lines in the snow on the Belgian front.

Above right: Pfc. Edward Brett, of Brooklyn, ties up wire for the 187th Field Artillery near Ligneuville, Belgium.

Bottom right: James Hilton, of Altamont, NY, tries out a new device for picking up wire. Hilton, from the 150th Armored Signal Company of the 10th Armored Division was demonstrating this device as early as February 5, 1945, when it became apparent that supply lines were stretched out and re-use of wire may be necessary, especially for the 3rd Army which was again on the move, without many of its trucks, which had been sent to Monty's armies.

back to Germany with their tanks between their legs. They, and the equipment they managed to take with them, escaped to kill again.

Montgomery was a great general: he studied, planned and consolidated better than most generals. It is fine that the British hold him in such high esteem, but not so fine that English writers pan Eisenhower and ignore Patton. Maybe there should have been a concerted push in one sector - but which one? Eisenhower was a diplomat. I would have chosen Patton's Third Army to be the one, in spite of all Monty's posturing. Eisenhower pleased most everybody, and got the job done. He did not please Montgomery or Patton. They both wanted to carry the ball. Frankly, I was underwhelmed by General Montgomery's use of overwhelming force, thereby taking time to build up for each attack and maybe alert the enemy, and, of course, the press. Maybe General Montgomery did have more opposition than Patton...because the enemy always knew that he was coming; and they were ready.

Montgomery moved forward methodically; Patton pushed forward with breakneck speed. Patton's Letters of Instruction to Corps, Division and Separate Unit commanders stated this axiom: "The farther forward the Command Posts are located, the less time is wasted in driving to and from the front. The ideal situation would be for the Army Command Post to be within one half hour's drive in a C & R car of the Division Command Post. The driving time to the front from the Command Post of the lower units should be correspondingly shorter.

A wireman from the 78th Infantry Division tests wire in the Lammersdorf-Rotgen sector. Troops had to contend with snow and cold weather as well as deadly artillery and mortar fire. Pulling artillery of the 309th within firing range required help from tanks of the Rainbow Division's accompanying 709th tank battalion to force the enemy beyond the assigned artillery position of the day. The 78th was "in the line" North of the 10th Armored Division; closer in the snowy Winter than in ensuing months.

"Much time and wire is saved if Command Posts of higher units are at or near one of the Command Posts of the next lower echelon." Third Army maintained two Command Posts, sometimes three. The forward one was more mobile. Patton's instructions state that it "should be kept as small and mobile as possible with the minimum amount of radio traffic." In Luxembourg, Patton's forward headquarters handled the bulk of Third Army communications, about 3,000 calls a day with four switchboard positions set up in a large moving van; one more than usual, plus another four inside headquarters!

Third Army headquarters was moved to a vacant seminary in Luxembourg in order to be close to the Battle of the Bulge. This large complex utilized additional power, furnished by Diesel-driven generators producing 50 Kilowatts, compared with the 10 Kilowatts of earlier operations. Originally the switchboard van had been wired to carry 300 pairs of wires, but that had been increased to 640. Use of this van helped to keep Patton's headquarters mobile and maintain communications at their peak.

At the installation the vans were arranged in the form of a rectangle so as to provide a covered runway between them. Their dusty stoves were removed and electric blowers installed, which, when they worked, reduced the cold somewhat. The area at the installation had to be policed constantly and the camouflage was checked daily.

It looked like the Luftwaffe knew a headquarters was in Luxembourg, probably due to the amount of radio traffic. They sent five planes over on December 30, but our fighters scrambled and a dog-fight ensued. Three enemy planes were downed and the other two went back the way they came. Our planes probably were called up from the air wing attached to Third Army. General Patton maintained tight control over use of this air wing, saving many a situation where something more than artillery was needed.

Of course, to maintain secrecy, the Third Army relied on wire when it was fresh, and quite heavily on messengers, or 'runners' as we called them. Sgt. James Clark, of Third Army Headquarters, said, "We had messengers that might take three days to deliver a mail pouch to another general. These were rigged to explode in case of capture. There was a metal box that the driver could activate, so that if an enemy would open the lid it would become a booby trap and all material inside would be destroyed." The messengers were now facing the most severe conditions...icy roads, snipers, blown bridges and black-out driving, but they got the messages through!

Artillery was not much of a factor in the ability of our messengers to get through, because artillery observers with the enemy infantry weren't close enough to our supply lines to get off a message in time to catch a fast-driving jeep.

On the other hand, it was important enough for Patton to list in his letters of instruction: "Sixty-five to seventy-five per cent of all artillery targets are provided by forward observers. The same percentage of tactical information originates with these observers, but much of the information the observers get comes from the infantry. Therefore, the forward observer must be in intimate association with the infantry. He must be under the control of the artillery liaison officer with the battalion. Artillery officers with infantry do not return to their batteries at night."

The forward artillery observer, previous page, is in touch with his battery by radio and wire. In fact, the feet of Jim Burns, wireman from the 94th Infantry, can be seen resting above the muddy floor of the foxhole as he reclines in a connecting trench. Shortly after this picture was taken, both antennas of the SCR300 radios were bro-

Don Young and Frank Armbuster in Metz.

Our 2 1/2 ton truck was pressed into service when the 10th Armored took more than three towns in one day, sometimes arriving in town before our tanks had cleared the other end. Here, road and rubble were streaked with drifting snow, and artillery or air support, or both, was in evidence. (Courtesy of Elwood Morecraft.)

Every time we passed through the bridge check-point at Thionville, we noticed an anti-aircraft gun, or ack-ack, as we called them. This photo, taken on January 21, shows Nicholas J. D'Arula of the 550th AAA on plane alert at the bridge. Another name for the gun he is handling is the Quad-50. These guns were quite mobile and were often used to suppress an enemy counter-attack.

Snow helped to camouflage Signal Vans at 3rd Army's Luxembourg Headquarters.

Morris Middleton and Patton.

Montgomery and Patton.

ken by shrapnell from an 88 shell. Jim explains that they had to use a lot of wire. "It was quicker to run a new line for up to 500 yards...better than stopping to expose two of us while repairing it."

In his Letter of Instruction No. 2, Patton points out that an armored unit should get in back of the enemy: "Battles are won by frightening the enemy. Fear is induced by inflicting death and wounds on him. Death and wounds are produced by fire. Fire from the rear is more deadly and three times more effective than fire from the front, but to get fire behind the enemy you must hold him by frontal fire and move rapidly around his flank. Frontal attacks against prepared positions should be avoided if possible." With the Siegfried line in front of us, however, we had to have a breakthrough before our armor could rush through the opening!

Patton would rush armor to a breakthrough even if we were 50 to 100 miles away! Another of his instructions, "The larger and the more violence you use in the attack, whether it be men, tanks, or ammunition, the smaller will be your proportional losses," in no way offset our method of taking a town with a couple of recon tanks. After all, we are just probing...like a surgeon removes a bullet...then we sew up the town with some of our larger tanks.

Our light tanks would go 35 to 40 miles per hour; the heavier Shermans 24 to 26 m.p.h. The Germans couldn't get used to our speed, and I don't think other generals knew how to cope with it. Patton did. Patton would get us running around in back of the enemy's lines until the gas ran out. Meanwhile, in

March 13, 1945: An 8-inch howitzer of Battery C 243rd Army Field Artillery Unit fires at an enemy observation post across the Sarr River from Bedersdorf, Germany. (Courtesy of Patton Library.)

the northern sector, Montgomery was wallowing in gas. Maybe that's a strong word, but he was actually building up, so he had to have a lot of gas, and it would look bad if we didn't let him have it.

Now we hear, 50 years later, that his style was cramped by not being allowed to go ahead. It could be that Patton's method of operation was cramped because Montgomery got more than his share of the gas and just sat on it while he prepared for one of his lavish breakthroughs. Actually, they weren't breakthroughs because he advanced with caution after he 'broke through.' Patton stressed speed. It became an advantage. Monty liked preparation. Too elaborate, it was a disadvantage.

General Montgomery failed to pinch off the bulge at the Falaise Gap battle; and he did the same thing at the Bastogne Bulge, in both cases allowing thousands to escape. Compared to the Fourth Armored, which cut North by bringing up artillery when their tanks got in trouble, Montgomery didn't move until a mass of artillery was in place. The Fourth Armored went twice as far to relieve Bastogne, fighting into the heavy opposition of surrounding Panzer divisions. Monty meanwhile won many battles with armies at his disposal, while advancing at a snail's clip.

The situation before General Montgomery's push South to meet Patton's troops was apparent to me only after a study involving both sides of the story. Those lauding the British general praised him for a thoughtful and tactical pause, enabling him to receive replacements and be at full strength. This is true, except that he waited for replacements for the U.S. Seventh Armored, which had borne the brunt of the Nazi arrowhead. One of the problems with history is that some of the best military history courses are at prestigious British universities!

Preparation seems logical until you delve into the matter a bit more, as the English might say. Then you realize Monty was saving 'his' troops for his next push. Patton wanted to do that, but followed orders, even volunteering to get help to Bastogne right away, which he did.

General Montgomery had temporarily been put in charge of General Hodges armies, but although British Divisions were also at low strength, they could have moved at once to cut off the Bulge. Some of his tanks were a good match for the Germans. They were Shermans on which the British had installed heavier guns. It seemed that he knew how to do it, and what to do, but did not master 'when.' The British troops were some miles to the North but it might have taken just a few days to get down to Houfallize. But waiting for replacements took a lot longer. Waiting for gas was not the issue. Neither was it necessary to wait for ammunition; so it must have been replacements. It ended up taking 28 days for Hodge's army to meet Patton's and complete the encirclement. Montgomery was too good a general to have just waited for the right moment. That moment may have never come. Why it was almost a month 'til General Hodge made the connection is anybody's guess, but only Monty to know.

Patton would have found a way to move his divisions, in...an hour? A day? By now his divisions were under-manned, but still had the firepower to stop the German retreat.

The public relations people could always find Montgomery. History books are full of his greatness! Patton has often been criticized by British authors for not preparing properly. Balderdash! Patton was ahead of his time. He was even ahead of the Blitzkrieg method, and understood it better than any general of his day. He stated "When the roads are available for use, you save time and effort by staying on them until shot off."

This statement can be misconstrued to mean for armor to run blindly at the enemy. When you delve into his whole outlook you realize that he is talking about probing. Why set up a whole artillery barrage and infantry division support when there may only be one enemy squad in the town? Looking at the entire picture, our recon tankers could take towns and capture a squad or platoon of Germans. We would be on them before they knew it, and many American lives were saved. Once in a while we would lose a tank or two and it was time to prepare for a battle at that town.

In effect, many lives were saved, and the enemy division, maybe headquartered in the next town to the side had to move out or be enveloped, because they had been out-flanked. It would seem reasonable that your flank is protected if an infantry division is coming up after your division.

When you look at the complete picture of Patton's Tactical Rules, it becomes clear that you cannot take one of his many pronouncements out of context. Just the way he ran his Third Army Headquarters was misunderstood.

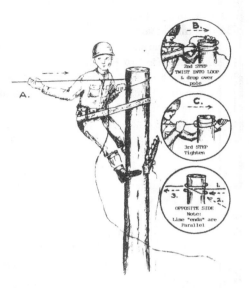

Lineman starts a Clove Hitch... faster than the usual pull-through slip knot.

Typical wireman action, but special signalman. One of the 30th Infantry Division wiremen, photographed by Jack Kitzerow a month earlier putting wire overhead at Geromont, Belgium during a counter-attack by the 30th. One of their men survived being machine-gunned in the Malmedy Massacre.

The 'spit-and-polish' attitude of the Third Army was misunderstood by many. It was known by the enemy, and the Third Army was feared. It looked to them like it was nothing for us to do battle with them. They understood discipline. A timely salute indicated to General Patton that his troops were alert, and that alertness might save their lives.

The quick way Third Army responded to events gained the respect of the Germans. Patton's armor always appeared in time to get the battle over with in our favor. He stated his policies repeatedly with mention of motion and speed. One of his statements discloses that fact: "Catch the enemy by the nose with fire and kick him in the pants with fire emplaced through movement." Here again, he was talking about getting to the rear of the enemy.

His headquarters was up to the task. They set up sand tables to be able to visualize terrain so they knew where to expect an attack, or where to initiate one. According to the general, "Sand tables need not be complicated - a piece of ground in the lee of a building is just as good and much simpler."

Communications were of utmost importance to Patton. His instructions pointed out what to do, and what not to do: "Don't place large radio sets near CP's if the CP is to be in position more than six hours. If radios must be used for longer periods, put them well away, scatter them, and use remote control." Officers of the 150th pressed this point. I believe our methods of using remotes from our complex radio halftracks were used as an example of how to use and install a remote.

We found this axiom to be a life-saving one. Also, because radio vehicles were so valuable, it was easier to protect them by using a remote. We could place them in a position that might be hard to get to, like next to a window instead of a door subject to shelling. We were able to both start and operate the radio track with our remote.

As for wire, Patton instructed us to "Push wire communications to the limit. A wire phone is worth three radios for both speed and security." It took as many radio operators in action as it did wiremen because they had to take turns.

EVERYWHERE WE GO
Wire, wire everywhere
But not a reel to spare.
We lay it with a certain flair
Wherever we may go.
We try to get it in the air
On pole or tree, but never low
Unless we may prevent a snare
By placing wire beside a wall;
Or fling it high to window ledge
And tie it so it will not fall
Along the street, where shells may land
Annoying tanks just up ahead;
So we can't end our wire as planned...
Especially when the tanks have fanned
Out around the town and fire
That tends to seek out
Tanks and jeeps and wire.

With Combat Command "B" back in the fold, a battle started to shape up. The 90th Infantry Division had been holding fast while the Krauts were kicking themselves against the Bastogne bastion. The 90th had forged the bridgehead above Thionville and weren't about to let it go!

The 90th was relieved by the 94th Infantry Division, who would be with us to help pave the way to Trier. It was hilly country, abounding with stone farm houses and flowing streams. There was still snow on the ground. In this area we could not use a swath of tanks, rather a file of tanks. With one tank at a time going up a draw, we presented an inviting target to the defenders, but it was necessary to support the infantry. Usually the infantry supported us, which is how it looked on paper.

However, we could not just wait for the 94th to spring us through the Siegfried Line. Both divisions fought like Tigers, to coin a phrase.

Patton maintained that there was not good or bad tank terrain...that tanks can and should operate anywhere. We certainly did that!

Some of the towns we had taken, in conjunction with the 90th Division had to be taken again. The Germans were still hanging on in the hills. One of these towns was Sinz, where the Germans had been defeated once before. They had moved back into town and commanded the hills above, and the 94th had to put up quite a fight to overcome the stubborn enemy. It was brought to my attention that the 80th Infantry Division had also taken a whack at Sinz before receiving orders to swing to a different section of the "front".

Herb Ridyard, in the 2nd Battalion of the 301st Regiment carried messages for his company of the 94th Division. He tells about the trouble they had at Sinz: "I had to lead an officer up to an advanced position at night. We had come to the edge of a woods where we saw a burning U.S. tank. Then an artillery burst caused us to look for a safer place than

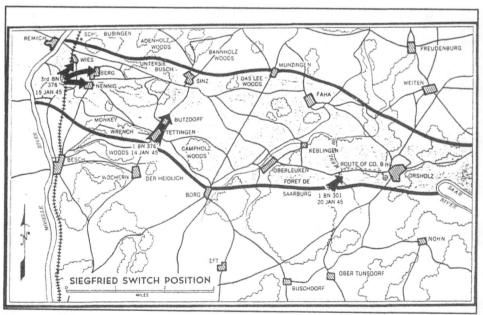

You can see how tough it was by the above map. We found it was next to impossible to just run a tank through. It took an infantry division, interfacing with tanks, to blast through any section, one pillbox at a time. Artillery had to have rifle trajactory to have an effect on some of the cement monsters, and it was difficult to get near enough to roast them out with flamethrowers. (Courtesy of 94th Infantry Division.)

10th Armored tank offers protection to 94th Infantry Division at Schilingen on the Siegfried Line. (Courtesy of 94th Infantry Division.)

The town of Sinz had been fired upon by several German divisions and several 3rd Army divisions. You can see by this photo that it took atillery, tanks and infantry working together to do the job. You can also guess that a certain number of bombing runs hit the town from time to time! Finally, notice the path of an uphill battle. (Courtesy of 94th Infantry Division.)

under trees where shells would explode before they hit the ground. I knew of an abandoned observation post so I led the way, hoping I could find it. I was actually glad to fall in the hole. It made me look good to find it in the middle of the night, so I didn't mind a few bruises. We had the spot for our dawn attack."

The 301st and other infantry regiments of the 94th Division finally broke through. Germans maintaining this section must have been worn to a frazzle. They started to come out of the pillboxes with their hands up, instead of dying to the last man. At that point the Tenth Armored hit the line like a fullback and we were on our way to the Saar River at a point close to Trier.

The men of the 94th had learned the same lesson that Patton taught his troops: 'To advance forward out of artillery fire' because artillery moves forward. They had also taken over a couple of pillboxes which helped to stem a counterattack by a defending division, and give our big guns time to go against their artillery in the rear.

It had snowed, and the tanks and moving men were easy to see, but many of their guns had been knocked out. Other enemy divisions had been pulled back across the Saar, where they waited for us. We would soon be there.

We worked hand-in-hand with the 94th during the drive on Trier. Both divisions were making their objectives. Whether General William Morris, Jr., 10th Armored, meeting with General Harry J. Malony, of the 94th Infantry Division; or by battle plans from Patton's Third Army Headquarters, the coordination went well, according to 94th Division documents:

"Following issuance of the attack order, the regimental commander (of the 94th's 376th Combat Team, attached to the 10th Armd. to attempt a crossing of the Saar on the morning of February 22) decided to conduct a personal reconnaissance of the crossing site beyond Ayl and at the same time to select a CP location within the town. As his jeep rolled down the hill toward town, movement could be seen through the darkness on the road ahead. The driver slowed his vehicle, expecting to be challenged by an American sentry. Then, one of the figures in the road became silhouetted - the distinctive outline of a German helmet was clearly visible. Luckily, the enemy was as startled as the colonel and his driver. Returning to Mannebach, Colonel McClure contacted the 10th Armored Division Headquarters and was informed that the armored infantry was about to take the town of Ayl."

During the afternoon of the 22nd, General Patton visited our 10th Armored Headquarters, more-than-politely inquiring why the crossing had not been made. By that time, enough assault boats had arrived, but the morning mist was missing, so smoke makers were brought into play. Enemy artillery demolished the landing craft, but more arrived and the crossing was finally made.

Moving up 94th Division

Top: 180th Engineer Battalion of 94th Infantry Division contend with Moselle ice floes while salvaging Bailey bridge at Apach. (Photos courtesy of Patton Library.)

Left: Farther South, at Saarlautern, the 320th Engineer battalion of the 95th Division puts foot bridge over the Saar.

Right: Soldiers of 94th Infantry Division look over chateau they captured at Nenning.

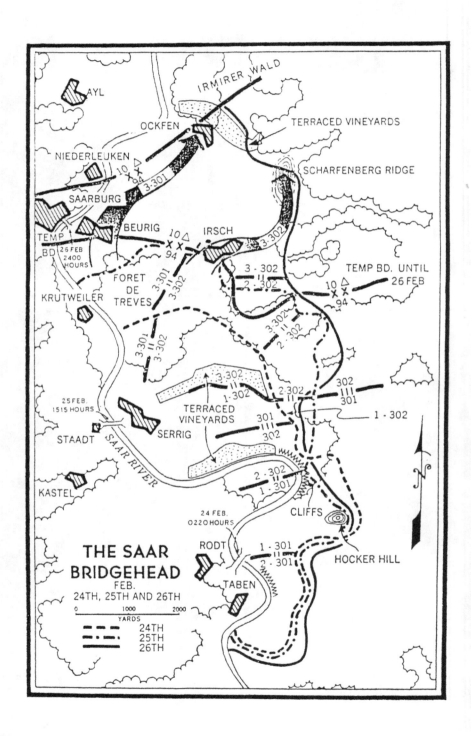

AYL

IRMIRER WALD

OCKFEN

TERRACED VINEYARDS

NIEDERLEUKEN

10 △
X
94
3-301

SCHARFENBERG RIDGE

SAARBURG

BEURIG

10 △
X X
94

IRSCH

3-302

TEMP
BD

26 FEB
2400
HOURS

FORET
DE
TREVES

3-301
3-302

3-301
3-302

3 - 302
||
2 - 302

TEMP BD. UNTIL
26 FEB

10 △
X X
94

KRUTWEILER

3-301
||
3-302

3-302
||
2-302

3-302
||
1-302

3-302
||
2-302

302
||
301

25 FEB.
1515 HOURS

TERRACED
VINEYARDS

2-302
||

1 - 302

STAADT

SERRIG

301
||
302

SAAR RIVER

KASTEL

24 FEB.
0220 HOURS

2 - 302
||
1 - 301

CLIFFS

RODT

1 - 301
||
2 - 301

HOCKER HILL

THE SAAR
BRIDGEHEAD
FEB.
24TH, 25TH AND 26TH

TABEN

0   1000   2000
YARDS

– – –   24TH
– · – ·   25TH
———   26TH

N

Combat Command "A" of the 10th Armored approached from the North, after an 'end-around' run to take the town of Ayl. That set the stage for the battle, and gave us a hilltop observation post and command center. The map on page 80 shows the logistics of the river crossing.

According to our records, it was February 23. The River Saar had sucummed to the web-footed engineers. Patton's concern at this time was noted in The Patton Papers. With the Tenth Armored spearheading the drive on Trier his diary of February 23 noted: "SHAEF has a new toy called SHAEF Reserve, and every time they let an Army have a division, they want one in return. Now they say that if I keep using the 10th Armored, I will have to put the 11th, 6th or 4th Armored in reserve - despite the fact that all these divisions are properly placed to attack. I just hope something will turn up to prevent my having to do this. The best I could do for the moment was to settle for 48 hours more time.

"Bradley called to state that I would get two new infantry divisions but would have to pull out two old ones in the so-called reserve."

At the time, it didn't look like we were to be used for the one last great armored advance in the southern sector. This became more apparent after looking at the records of Patton's involvement with the armored division training and supply. Even our signal company had 2 1/2-ton trucks to send back for wire if we had to, and Division Quartermaster had the 132nd Ordnance Maintenance Battalion to repair our vehicles.

Compared to the time it took German divisions to get new equipment, it must have seemed like a miracle to them. Martin Urich, formerly of the German tank corps, said that he had to stay with his tank during World War II to wait for parts, which were late in coming. Two months later, still waiting, he had to surrender. He had stayed with his tank, as required, but his position was over-run. You can bet our bombing raids had something to do with that! After the war, Urich was able to come to the United States. He became a sergeant in the U.S. Army and recently retired. Undoubtedly, his experience was helpful.

We were about to establish our reputation as a division. A lot of this had to do with Patton's planning. We took a whack at the Siegfried Line, participated in the Battle of the Bulge, and still managed to help him conduct a major breakthrough, starting with the Trier engagement.

Patton's tank divisions were always running out of gas, yet up North, near Aachen, piles of gasoline were missed by the Germans during their breakthrough, and thousands of gallons had to be ignited to keep them out of the hands of the Nazis. Why weren't more gallons alloted to Patton's Army? He was one of the few who understood modern warfare, but was held back in deference to a unified front!

In February, after helping to clear out the Saar-Mozelle triangle, town-by-town, we were called on to advance from Faulquemont, France, to Ayl, Germany, a distance of about 71 miles. Suddenly, we appeared at the Siegfried Line with the 94th Infantry Division.

The German 19th Army was stationed on the North side of the Siegfried Line, which juts out roughly 90 degrees from the Saar. Instead of helping clean out the pocket, we were racing to find a way over the Saar. It had taken an extra month of mopping up until we were released for Patton's last push.

Tenth Tanks Take Trier

Ardent advance across Saar River at Serrig

Tenth Armd. & 94th Div.

90th Div.
76th Div.
Ehrang 3/6/45
KYLE
10th captures Romer Bridge from the East side! 3/1
TRIER 3/1
Fell
55th Armored Eng. clear mines
Karthaus
Konz
Filsch 2/28
Pluwig
Oberbillig
Tawern
Wiltingen
Pellingen 2/28
Reinsfeld
Roodt
2/23
Ayl
C.C.A. C.C.B.
Heameskell
Oetrange
Wincheringen 2/21
2/21
Ockfen
Irsch
Zerf 2/27
SAARBURG
Serrig 2/23
Weiskirchen
Palzem
Trussem
11/22
Sinz 90?
Munsingen
Freudenburg
Wadern 3/18
Nenning
MAIN 94th Div.
Weiten
PRIMS
Besch
Tettingen
Borg 11/21
Mettlach
Losheim
MOSELLE
Orsholz
SAAR
Nunkirchen
11/21
Perl
APACH & 2/18
Silwingen
MERZIG
Sierck
Waldwisse
Beckingen
Laumsfeld 11/16
Halstroff
Monneren
La Croix
THIONVILLE
Yutz
11/1
Filstroff 11/19
Dalstein
Bouzonville
Freistroff 12/24 (Tanks)
NIED

2/24
Liaison planes of 5th Ranger Bn. of 94th Div. drop supplies at bridgehe Both 94th Div. and 55th Armd. Engineer build bridges

CHAPTER 8

ARTILLERY AT TRIER

PATTON AT THE GATES OF TRIER
Give me the Tenth Armored
And the Saar-Moselle triangle
Is mine. No more will bored
Wehrmacht Nazis sit and wrangle
Over spoils of war, nor
Dance and feast at Trier, and jangle
Their swords and medals for
Mock adoration of all.
Our troops knock at the gates
Of the town which soon will fall.
Secure, the city waits;
Knowing not the coming pall.

No matter what conditions we faced, we laid wire from the new field unit positions to the new Division Headquarters location each day; and got it in place before dark. These commands, in turn, would lay finer lines up to their units. We repaired our wire, but the infantry units, under direct fire, would just run another line, dodging bullets on the way. There would be less exposure than if they stayed to fix it.

Throughout the campaigns, our switchboard would establish what we called a "Radio City" where operators would run remotes to their specially-equipped radio tracks. We would run lines from there to combat commands. A write-up from the Historical Report of the 150th Armored Signal Company explains this tactic. It refers to the hilltop town of Ayl:

"Wire was generally kept to all combat commands while in the process of clearing the triangle between the Saar and Moselle rivers. The radios were located on the highest terrain feature in the vicinity of the division C.P. The results were good radio communication. At times, this radio city was located some distance from other troops and additional infantry guard was used for protection at night.

"The next phase of the operation was the capture of Trier, Germany. This involved a division crossing of the Saar River and then a very narrow drive parallel to the front on into Trier. A regimental combat team attached to the division made an assault crossing of the river and established a small bridgehead. The infantry of the division was dismounted and crossed by ferry when it was found impossible to build a bridge in the face of heavy artillery and sniper fire from pillboxes."

Of course, our own artillery was answering back, and the whine of smaller shells and the whoosh of larger ones, both outgoing and incoming, played a music of anxiety to our brains. To the tune of Old McDonald, Hoby sang, "With a krump, krump, here and a krump, krump..." We said, "Shut up."

I remember vividly when we took the famous old wine distribution city of Trier near the junction of the Saar and Moselle rivers. It looked like we were headed toward the city, but missed a concentration of enemy artillery by heading Southeast along the Saar River (see map). German artillery had zeroed in on the road where the Tenth Armored approached beyond the hilltop village of Ayl. South of the village, which we used as a command

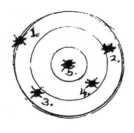

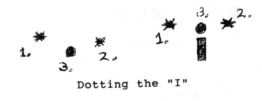

Dotting the "I"

Bracketting

REVOLUTIONARY WAR   WORLD WAR II

center, accompanying infantry was subject to artillery fire as they plodded on, in single file, spread out on both sides of the road. Even from the flat area below the town I could see many German vehicles retreating bumper-to-bumper up a long hill on the opposite side of the river, heading South, away from Trier.

Their artillery had been ready to blast us at a crossing East of Trier, but we outsmarted them by swinging South to attempt a crossing further upstream. (The river flowed in a northerly direction.) This move would have trapped the Germans, so they struggled away from Trier, while we kept up with the nearest arm of their division, with only the fast-moving river between.

We had already taken thousands of prisoners, trapped in the river triangle on this side, and we moved quickly to try for another entrapment. Some of their artillery must have been outpaced, but they were still very strong. Obviously, additional guns had been moved up. Evidently they were using an accurate bracketing technique.

General Von Steuben used 5-shot bracketing in our Revolutionary War to train 5-cannon batteries. Now, if a shell missed on the left, then again on the right, chances are it would hit on the third try.

Everything we did was related to the river crossing. Even equipment was brought up for the radio sets, as noted in our Company History: "Also during this operation, it was necessary to establish a small signal dump immediately adjacent to planned river crossing. This was necessary because troops making assault crossing had little transportation and required many batteries to use in operation of portable sets."

Infantry from the 94th Division was helping to exploit the beachhead, and the enemy was being pushed back to the point where they could not fire directly into the landing craft except with their artillery. However, they still commanded the hilltops. We were through one section of the Siegfried Line, but still had the river to bridge.

Enemy big guns were beyond the hill, blasting our pontoon bridge South of Saarburg. Word came over our forward line, "The bridge has been blown." That night, engineers used this site as a decoy and moved the bridge further South, while infantry maintained the bridgehead. One of our crews had rowed across the river and proudly presented our line to an infantry lieutenant. They were under fire - well, the whole area around the river bank was under fire. The command post was behind a tree and an overturned assault boat. When the coil of wire was handed to the lieutenant his words were (and I quote this as accurately as possible), "I don't want this #x!*@ line - you're too early."

Maybe he thought it would draw more enemy fire! Some officer in our division - or company - was trying too hard to emulate Patton. The Company History noted it like this:

"Wire was put across the river - assault wire, W-110-B and spiral 4 cable, the latter proving the best. Continuous artillery made relaying the circuits a continuous operation.

"To supplement this communication, an SCR-300 was remoted from a hill to the C.P., approximately 400 yards. This provided excellent communication to a combat command, one mile over the river, but required frequent battery changes. Frequent artillery made it necessary to remote all radios to cellars or dugouts. To insure cooperation between division artillery and attached artillery, signal company radios were sent out to attached artillery units.

"The original bridge plan was abandoned and a southern crossing was made successfully."

We had laid the wire out in a field away from the road which was bordered with columns of infantry from the 94th Division, moving up to the new bridgehead on the other side of Saarburg. Hoby and I were driving up in our crew's wire jeep to shoot trouble on the line. Shells were exploding on the road, but the troops continued to move, walking at intervals to avoid losing more than one or two men to an accurate artillery burst. When we saw a couple of G.I.'s on the ground, with men continuing around them in single file, Hoby increased the speed of the jeep. We entered Saarburg at the same time the Krauts stepped up their bombardment.

Hoby jumped out of the jeep and entered a command post where we had set up a field phone. I ducked into the next door just as a 105 shell exploded in back of us. The beckoning entrance led immediately to a dirt-floor room where a squad of infantry had taken

General Patton matches his stars to the three on bridge over the Saur River; February 20, 1945. (Courtesy of Patton Library.)

85

shelter. As I started out the door one of them said kindly, noting my nervousness, "Why don't you sit down for a couple of minutes, the barrage is almost over." He was right. After about two minutes more of consecutive shelling, it was over. I found Hoby examining the jeep, which had escaped the shelling. He said, "You know, Don, one shell at a time isn't so bad, but that was fierce."

Columns of G.I.'s still plodded on. Medics were busy as they moved soldiers caught in the stepped-up shelling. We drove in silence, back out of town to the danger area where we thought the break would be.

When we approached the open area we parked the jeep in the field and walked until we found the break - out in the middle of the field. We thought it was far enough out when we laid it, but the incoming rounds had missed the road. Intent on our job, we proceeded to strip the wire, tie it in a square knot, wrap the ends around, and...just as we started to tape, an 88 fired at us, like a rifle, from the opposite hill. The whine the shell caused was pitched extremely high, so it couldn't have missed by much. Still holding the wire with both hands, I looked up from the ground, where I had dived in a hurry. Hoby was also looking up, still holding the tape. We were immobile for only a second or two, but it seemed like a moment frozen in time. Hoby didn't even have time to laugh.

When we relaxed enough to see each other laying on the ground, we simultaneously looked at the jeep, still intact; then Hoby wound the tape faster than I had ever seen it done. With one accord we sprinted 50 yards or more to the jeep before they could get off another round.

That splice must have done the trick. Lines were back in again. Better still, the Krauts must have run out of their ammunition allotment for the hour. We could move around without being bombarded.

Back in the shell-pocked town again, we learned that a friend of mine, Charles Young, had been hit in the leg with a piece of shrapnel while on K.P. and was being sent back to the states. The shell had landed just 40 feet from the open doorway where I had hesitated. I stepped gingerly around the spot of blood at the Mess Hall door. We were less jocular at mealtime, but were all too hungry not to eat.

Later that day, our halftrack was pressed into service to pick up a switchboard from Ayl. Word had come: "We're moving up." Our track lumbered up the hill into Ayl to the roar of incoming shells. The village boasted a commanding view of the Saar River, but we were too busy to see how the German retreat was coming along - up the other hill across the river. They were moving away, but their artillery was still coming in! We hurried up the hill because we had a job to do, not thinking that if we could see across the river, the Germans could watch us on the winding road. In retrospect, we should have parked in back of the switchboard building. Not only was it under observation, it was also under fire!

As Terry pulled up in front of a weathered building, a shell landed, showering us with dirt. The shrapnel missed. In a few seconds we sprinted down steps to the basement switchboard room, where Al Bruns had folded his switchboard, ready to go. We weren't quite as ready!

Just then a corporal from another unit burst into the room. "Our truck has been hit...OK if we go with you?" "Sure," we yelled. Another 105 hit outside. "Let's go now," someone shouted. There was no time to think about it. We ran up the steps, grabbing the switchboard on the way...before another incoming shell could find us...leaving the 2 1/2-ton truck in the street with a blown-up engine.Hopefully, the 132nd Ordnance Battalion would be able to put a new engine in the truck and get it going again.

Roman Bridge to Trier was captured intact by going "around" but graceful arches have since been replaced.

Folded umbrellas indicate a search for sun as sun-seekers enjoy a Fall day at rebuilt Saarburg.

Repainted, the village of Ayl sits atop a sharply-sloped hill South of Trier on the West side of the Saar.

That night we swept the broken glass aside and rolled our bedrolls out on the floor of a ground-level room. Cracked shutters let in the Winter winds and the noise from sporadic shelling, now more distant but clear in the night air.

The next morning, tanks had moved up and were crossing the pontoon bridge, skidding down the bank and then gingerly over the planks as the bridge sagged for each tank as they went forward in a wave. Shells were coming in less frequently. The Krauts were falling back to zero in on the next intersection under attack, ten miles beyond the river; and Trier. But we fooled them again! Now on the enemy side of the river, most of our division turned left and followed the river road to Trier. That way we could attack the next crossroads from two directions. One of our wire crews was lost - they didn't turn left.

Our Company History reports: "Wire was installed to an advance C.P. over the new bridge. As the advance C.P. moved North parallel to the Saar River wire could not always be put forward due to enemy infiltrations and considerable sniper fire from pillboxes. As a result radio traffic was heavy."

Other tanks, belching fumes, were waiting in fields North of Ayl, hidden by the shadow of the hill. They awaited their turn to run the gauntlet of artillery fire between Ayl and Saarburg, on their way to the pontoon bridge.

A 10th Armored tank fires, supporting infantry as they move house-to-house on a cobbled street in Trier.

When we swung North toward Trier, up the opposite side of the Saar, I thought we might be cut off against the river. None of the enemy brass realized this, although it was the third time we tried this maneuver. It proved to me that the German soldier may be able to follow orders very well, but did not act on his own initiative. We were up against the German 19th Army, with many veterans of the Russian front. Someone must have figured out what we were doing, and been in a position to, at least, harass us. Sniper fire was not enough!

Because CCA was in the forward position, our wire track followed the tanks into Trier. We located the communication center and found an open wire leading in from the edge of town, saving a lot of our wire in the process. One of us got up on the pole until our operator found the line we were hooked into with the field phone. The wire to other towns ahead of us had been cut earlier.

It became our turn to rest up for one or two nights on the outskirts of Trier. Some of the men took a jeep into town to pay a "visit" to the famous wine cellars which had been turned over to the French and were now guarded by them. We figured they would be amenable to our request for a few bottles of champagne. They were. They even helped our men pick out several bottles! Our soldiers were pleased that the French guards were so friendly. Unfortunately, they picked green champagne. I wonder if maybe they knew what they were doing. Our men actually had green faces, which was quite unusual. They wanted to throw up, but couldn't. And they were in no position to complain. They weren't supposed to go into town. So that's the way it went. We took the town with its champagne vaults and couldn't get a decent drink.

Compared to obstacles we ran into at the river, Trier fell into our fold in an easy manner, as described by the Report: "During and subsequent to the capture of Trier, enemy communication systems were spotted and looked into while combat troops were approaching the installation. Prior to the actual capture of Trier, an underground cable was cut to destroy communication between that city and large cities to the South. In Trier, the telephone building was captured intact, by sending a halftrack and wire crew directly to it as combat elements entered town. A guard was posted to prevent unauthorized entry by saboteurs or American soldiers." (I'm sure none of our American soldiers were saboteurs.)

Artillery was a big factor in the Trier battle; not just incoming, but we answered them with our batteries positioned beyond the hills of Ayl. The enemy was shooting at our infantry, while our artillery was concentrating on knocking out their artillery.

Of course, the pontoon bridge was kept under fire until our beachhead could be expanded. By the time we reached Trier, their artillery had pulled back in fear of being outflanked. We knew our tanks would bypass the next intersection, which was bound to be zeroed in by the enemy 105's.

A good explanation of how an artillery battalion worked was offered by Don DiMarco, Sr., of West Chester. He was chief gunner for his battery of the 309th Field Artillery, who fought with the 78th Division in the Remagen Bridge sector. Ninth Armored tanks had scooted over the bridge before it could be blown and the resulting bridgehead needed the reinforcement heavy artillery could offer. His outfit consisted of 155 howitzers. "Their shells weighed 98 lbs., so our service trucks had to make many trips back to the ammunition dump at Aachen, Belgium," disclosed Sgt. DiMarco. "It was the morning of December 16th that we really found that we were in the front lines fighting a war," noted the History of the 309th Field Artillery Battalion.

"A four-man gun section was wiped out because roots were in the way of digging foxholes," stated DiMarco. "Other men flattened out in deep tank tracks nearby. It wasn't long before we contacted a nearby cavalry group who had shot an azimuth to the enemy guns. They in turn called another outpost to get a second reading. We blasted back at them on a count-down, with help from the adjacent battery from the 102nd."

When the 309th got into position they were set to use the "X-ray" fuse which explodes in mid-air. "We killed 96 with one barrage with this method," he said. The Battalion History listed several types of shells that were used at Merzenich: "The town had just been cleaned out four hours before and there were enemy troops in the next town three or four miles away. To help clean out that town, we fired our 'Kaput Special.' Some of the guns would fire an HE shell with a quick fuse to keep the Jerries inside and knock some buildings in a little. A couple other guns would fire HE shells with a fuse delay to blow the buildings apart. The other guns would fire white phosphorus shells with some quick fuses and some delayed fuses to set the place afire. To cross 'em up we would toss in a few Posit jobs to make sure they weren't out in the open too long trying to put out the fires. Later, before we moved out, our Infantry notified us that this type of fire was pretty effective."

Even though the bridge at Remagen was crossable, it was under heavy fire from German 105 batteries and bigger guns from eight or more miles away. "Engineers had built a pontoon bridge North of Remagen, so we crossed there to get close enough to help the expanding bridgehead. They had laid down a wide smoke screen to make it easier to cross, but it didn't seem too easy. German planes were strafing blindly through the smoke and artillery shells were probing for the bridge while we were crossing," DiMarco revealed. That sounds a lot like our Saar crossing, except that we didn't have a lot of strafing because of the hills.

MAKE-UP OF AN ARTILLERY BATTALION

A Battery	B Battery	C Battery	Headquarters	Service
Lt.+Forward Observers	Lt.+Forward Observers	Lt.+Forward Observers	Commanding Officers	
4 Howitzers each with Sergeant Gunner Corporal Powder Man 2 Loaders Ramrod Driver	4 Howitzers each with up to 8 men	4 Howitzers each with up to 8 men	2 Wiremen 2 Forward Observers 2 Radiomen Lt. Plane(s)	2 1/2-ton Trucks to make trips to the ammunition dump
	Each of these batteries had a Field Kitchen and a 2 1/2-ton truck to pick up shells from the Service Battery			

Large howitzers, like the 155's can, as a battery, fire over 300 rounds per hour while loading shells that weigh in at 98 lbs. each. By the time the 309th Field Artillery Battalion reached Mehlem, on the East side of the Rhine, they had logged over 30,000 shells! Each shell had to be followed by a powder charge, which determined the range. Although the heavy shells are supposed to be loaded by two men using a kind of stretcher, usually one or two of the stronger men would take turns as loader if the battery was firing as fast as possible.

In the case of a separate field artillery unit, like the 309th, wire would be run to

Gunner Watkins, of the 309th, hefts a 98-lb. shell into his 155 howitzer, normally a two man job. (By Don DiMarco, Sr.)

another accompanying Battalion Headquarters, to Service, and to all three batteries. Each battery would lay their own line to the Battalion Command Post. Headquarters would be responsible for a line to an adjacent artillery outfit, which might be already tied in to Division Headquarters. Depending on the topography or on the battle plan, each run of wire could be as much as five miles, for a total of 30 miles after all phones were in. Usually it was less. The 78th Div. would lay wire to them.

We had a lot of field artillery to bring to bear on the Germans. With the 10th Armored, we had 105's and also a component of 155's to help. If the resistance was tough, there was usually an Infantry Division nearby to lend a hand with their artillery. Sometimes it became a duel in the sun.

AT/302 men of 94th Infantry Division at Krefeld, Germany.

Chapter 9
THE GHOST DIVISION,
SPEARHEADS TO THE RHINE

The beginning of March found CCA mopping up along "our" side of the Moselle, going northeast (see map on next page). We continued to confuse the Germans as to the intent of the Tenth Armored when we swung out along the river to herd the enemy toward the river, cutting through on our way to they-knew-not-where. Then when we turned around and came back along a parallel set of towns, they had no where else to go except down to defeat. It was in this time frame that the Germans were starting to have second thoughts about being on the winning team.

When we started this route away from our command, there was a problem of communication with Division Headquarters. Evidently Col. Graham was following through with our usual ability to "keep wire communications." As a result of our position, it seemed highly likely that a wire across the Moselle from West to East would save miles and miles or wire as well as eliminating some radio messages that would give away our position.

The resulting creative effort by Sergeant Walker to put a line across the river was a good idea. Our wire jeep had met up with Walker's halftrack along the river. A rowboat was spotted. A couple of us volunteered to go because we could row, or swim...or both. Sgt. Walker said, "Since it's a project for my crew, I'll take one of my men." And out they went, without much ado, since it was getting late and an evening mist was rising from the swollen river.

The craft started out in calm waters near the shore. Farther out, we could see some current, which was soon obscured by the fog. We paid out the wire at a steady pace, so as not to disturb their ability to control the sluggish craft. We took turns with the wire, pulling it by hand. The river dragged at the line until we had a mile of wire out. At that point it was dark, and we hoped that they would cut the wire if they got into trouble. I don't think Sgt. Walker could swim. We never saw either of them again.

A LOST FRIEND
Sorrow is too deep for tears,
When one realizes loss.
Let your mind assay the fears
Of loneliness, and try to toss
Your head in laughter and song.
Weeping and sadness never gain
An inch of life, when life is gone.
It's pity for self until tears rain;
And sadness clouds the eyes and heart.
Your friend left 'cause God was ready;
Time had come for you to part.
So keep your soul and mind steady
Toward the time when you shall meet
On a highway in the Heaven,
For the aftermath of life is sweet.

During this push we were cut off on all sides. It was March 10th, in some small town that I got to write a letter home because we were there for an extra day, while supplies were being dropped to us from the air - gasoline, you can be sure! A Red Cross "coffee cart" had somehow made it into town and we had coffee and doughnuts until we got the call to move out. The Red Cross team included a couple of pretty women, volunteers, no doubt. I think they were going to put on a skit of some kind, but about that time we were bombed and they realized the reports that this area was in our hands were slightly overstated. They were leaning out of an upstairs window, but quickly ducked in.

It was one of Patton's rules that when a division came back in the same direction, it would attack on different terrain! We must have cleared out the area assigned to us, for t appeared we were soon headed in the opposite direction, but on back-country roads. German planes came at us, but resistance melted.

Since there were no large towns or cities of importance on this drive, it was not necessary to have another division alongside, although the 76th was nearby to help if needed.

After a short stint of mopping up, we were off to the southeast, toward St. Wende , with the 80th infantry as our flank protection, so we could by-pass or charge through the towns, whichever took less time. According to prisoners, we were starting to be called "The Ghost Division" by the Germans. This was the segment of battle that Patton revelled in - use of his armor in a free-wheeling manner! For those who have complained about his lack of flank protection at times, the above-mentioned fight forward, then fight back along a parallel road is a good answer. It just eats up the enemy! They don't know where you are, and have to jump out of the way, instead of zeroing in on where you might be! Of course the enemy had observers that would spot us and have a few shells lobbed in before they would retreat.

Now that we were off in a different direction, the enemy had to move troops around to try to stop us. There was a lot of talk about up North it was a lot tougher, in Monty land. All it was, was colder. Patton made it look easy by directing his Third Army to keep going. We didn't loose any more troops with this method than other armies, about one death to two for the enemy - and yet we took thousands of prisoners! Patton broke the "front" and could now use armor as it should be used, with tanks continuing to go forward until they get stuck...then bring the artillery to bear. Our mobile infantry kept up with the tanks. When they would lose some of their halftracks they would ride on the tanks. If there was room, men from the accompanying infantry division would also ride the tanks, affording protection for them and for us. At first, we didn't have room on the tanks, having lost a few vehicles, but as our infantry losses increased we gladly accepted any troops we could get.

It was necessary that the infantry jump off the tanks when we approached a road block or town. At that point they would not be "sitting ducks." They could move against the enemy infantry. Also, the turret machine gun could be swung from side-to-side if necessary. In a town, sniper fire was dangerous to our exposed tank commanders, who could see better when the turret was not buttoned down. If a sniper or machine gun nest was operating down the street while our tanks were plowing through, it was customary for the gunner to let loose a shell and blow a hole in the building to protect the infantry alongside.

Our 90th Reconnaissance Squadron had some open-top vehicles complete with tank tracks. They looked like a tank with no top. A 50-caliber machine gun rolled in a groove around the perimeter. Our recon tanks were lighter, but faster than the Shermans, so they could outflank a roadblock if possible. Now that we raced for the Rhine, our Recon Cavalry played an important part in our ability to blast through in a hurry.

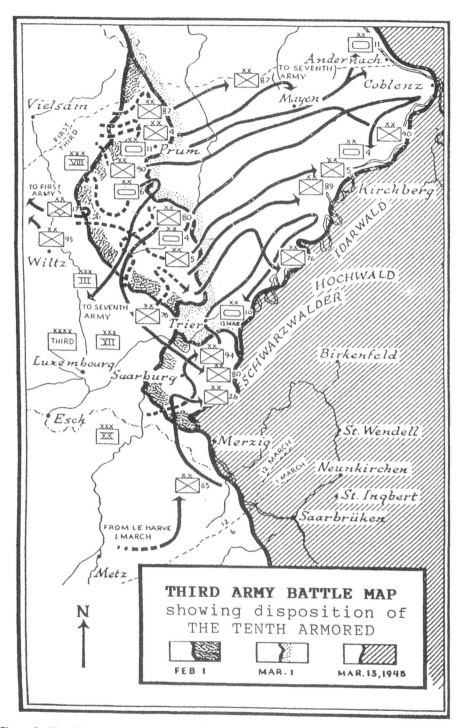

Since the Tenth Armored was "on loan" to Patton, Eisenhower's Headquarters wanted it back, but evidently settled for the Sixth because we were involved in an attack at the time. Note the Sixth was sent to the Seventh Army.

Even though the 10th Armored and the 80th Infantry divisions needed replacements, we fought on. The surprise we were affecting was worth more than a week of waiting for G.I. replacements to come up from the rear.

We also had to contend with an early March snowstorm. Wire was wet, and a little stiff from the cold, but we managed to tie our bow-release knots on the snow-plastered poles.

The wire jeep, at right, sported a large reel. We called them two-man reels. They could spin off a mile of wire, which stayed attached to the jeep until we needed to put on another full reel.

Other outfits opted for the half-mile reel, which one man could easily lift in place, but which required twice as much splicing. We were glad we selected the heavier reels. They stayed in place on our welded double-height racks and afforded additional protection from shrapnel bursts alongside. Every man in our crew could lift the large reels off the rack and heft it in place, but we usually needed help in getting it on the axle. Each crew had a halftrack

(Courtesy of Buddy Lovette, 165th Signal Photo Company.)

and a jeep. Terry, our track driver, was able to relax better than the rest of us, fortunately, because we didn't need an up-tight driver.

At night we had a small radio to listen to, and would have friendly arguments over what kind of music to play. Frank and I liked classical, but Terry went for the hillbilly tunes. One night Hap was listening to Count Basie: "I Left My Love in Salt Lake City." He says to Frank, jokingly, "Shut up so I can hear the music." Frank says, "Well, just listen to me, I'm singing the same thing." Oh yes, tonight we have champagne that we found in the cellars. We continue to listen to the music. Most of the time the only kind of music we can get is classical or accordion, so this is a real treat, not to mention the champagne. Hopefully we won't have to shoot any trouble on this cold night.

Another driver was acquired for one of our new weasels. Hamp fit in with our crew, and we welcomed Corb back. Now we were set for mud and streams. I wondered if the weasel could do better than our jeep with its four-wheel drive. One day we got stuck trying to ford a stream with the jeep. The mud bogged us down, but the winch on the front was able to pull us out. We all ended up with wet feet, which was nothing new.

Believe me, we had it just as tough as anybody trying to get through the Siegfried line, as several divisions know who tried it. Now things were going a little easier because the Germans didn't know which way we were headed. When the pivotal town of Kaiserslautern loomed on the horizon, things changed. We were encountering some mines on the autobahn. While zig-zagging through branches that we thought were broken off by artillery, our halftrack lost a front wheel to an exploding mine. Fortunately, no one was hurt and we were able to get going again. We all piled in the jeep and left the halftrack for our 132nd Ordnance to pick up. All they had to do was fix a tire. We went a lot slower in the jeep.

The enemy was moving troops in our path, now that they had figured out our direction. After Kaiserslautern, where the 80th division stayed to subdue the town, we curved South to Landau and the Rhine. One account of the intervening road to Landau is related by Mario S. Endrizzi, who was a sergeant with our 90th Recon Battalion at St. Martin's woods. "Late in March the Squadron, in a piecemeal column swung out of Kaiserslautern, Germany and headed for the Rhine. On the point an assault gun from Easy Troop rolled along a road cluttered with the wreckage of the fleeing Krauts, and it wasn't long before we met up with our arch-enemies. It was one of those days when, instead of defending to the last their sacred soil, they preferred to drink wine and champagne and be happy. They had beaucoups of the stuff, looted in Igolsbach. When we came up to them, they readily surrendered and even promised to look for pistols for us. We declined the offer of the pistols (being well up on the art of pistol finding), but we officially liberated the drink'n stuff.

"In Igolsbach we were joined by a platoon from 'F' Company. Our task force now consisted of one platoon each from 'F', 'D', and 'E' Troops. F's platoon took the lead on a road leading to a town called St. Martin.

"It was the steepest, darkest, wind'nest road we had ever seen, and although Krauts were suspiciously absent, their just-abandoned equipment was everywhere. There was a burning German ammunition wagon that exploded and blew one of 'D' Troop's armored cars over the steep embankment. By some miracle the crew got out of the inferno, but two Heinie prisoners weren't so lucky. Pinned underneath the wreckage, they died. A second explosion and one of our assault guns was flung to the side - half over the embankment. Somehow between the flaming armored car and the exploding wagon, men's minds func-

The 150th Armored Signal Company received three new weasels the beginning of March, just in time for the Spring thaw, so we could lay lines out along streams and field-ends to by-pass rows of trees and poles. Frank Armbuster looks out of the vehicle, while two men from another crew stand by, after transferring a wire reel to their jeep.

tioned and the crew managed to move the lumbering tank. Maybe the champagne cargo inspired them. (It tasted good to us.)

"Things quieted down a bit until an 88 popped up. We had picked up a Belgian civilian along the way, and he offered to talk the Krauts into surrender. Evidently he didn't convince them, because they shot him. That started the fireworks. Captain Anderson blew up the gun, and the Germans knocked out the lead tank with panzerfaust fire. Sgt. Giaquinto from Easy Troop took the lead, and in the next mile his gunner, Corporal August, knocked out two anti-tank guns, a bunch of Panzerfausts, and machine gun nests. By this time the rest of the Squadron had swung into the tempo, and from the racket it sounded as if the entire ETO and CBI fronts were zeroing in on the St. Martin woods. Most of the 90th (without 16 weeks of basic) was quickly converted into foot infantry. We looked in the book, but the advice wasn't too sound.

Patton stakes a claim on Germany. (Courtesy of Patton Library.)

"It was Colonel Lichirie who turned out to be the man of the day. He gave an impromptu speech in German and won quite a number of Krauts' hearts. By that time it was almost pitch black, so we decided to spend the night in the forest primeval. The night was quiet in its fashion, but we sweated harder than a guy with 300 points. Everything that moved and everything that didn't move was Kraut. Around three o'clock Sgt. Giaquinto let go with his thirty. In the dawns's early light we found a headless Heinie with a potato masher still in his hand not twenty feet away from the tank.

"In the blazing morning sun we roared into St. Martin's narrow, crooked streets. There was a little rear guard action, but the bulk of the enemy forces had withdrawn toward the bridgeless Rhine.

"The front suddenly rushed on ahead, and we were left in St. Martin for almost a day to get off the grime and shaky feeling of the past night, and for the occasion that liberated liquid loot was prima."

Such was the way our Recon Squadron operated! I'm sure that the 4th Armored operated that way...blasting through towns without the benefit of the heavier Shermans. The Tenth fought our way down to Landau before the Germans really got a fix on our division. It was March 22nd. This was the night the 5th Infantry Division crossed the Rhine. By the next day they had a beachhead established miles wide and just as deep; permitting one of Patton's staff to read a "modest" announcement, ostensibly from Patton praising his troops for crossing with little fanfare and without the benefit of artillery. Without saying so, this referred to Montgomery's lavish display, a day later, complete with banks of artillery and hundreds of airplanes...and all observed by Churchill. Patton must have had a laugh when Churchill praised the British troops for being the first ones over the Rhine! Actually, the Ninth Armored was first over the Rhine at Remagen.

The grapevine told us that Patton had reached the Rhine. Rumors say he swam the Rhine but I know that what Patton did to indicate possession was what wolves do to mark their territory. He watered the Rhine.

PATTON'S WATERING

Patton urged his men
To cross by boat - or swim
If fire fell too close.

The day was hot and dim;
And shells were "coming in"...
Ask anyone who knows...
How Patton led his faithful men
Into the smoke and battle's din.

The chill of Winter still remained
Between the river's banks...
And on our side the tanks
Were waiting on a country lane.

While Patton watered the river Rhine
With men who knew this was the sign:
A bridge would soon be "thrown across"
In snow or sleet or rain.

My uncle, who had many connections with photographers in New York, had in his possession a photograph of Gen. Patton taken during his "watering." Taken from the flank, the photo exhibited only the stream of "water," but was unmistakably of the General himself, complete with white-handled side arms and Eisenhower jacket. He stood, surrounded by his staff, on the bank of a great river. A more frontal view on page 98 proves the point. Patton always did what he said he would do.

J. Hubert Sanders, of our 21st Tank Battalion, comments on his experience at the Rhine: "Our tank was the first Tenth Armored tank to cross at Worms on the pontoon bridge. We got three of our Shermans across before the bridge was blown up, leaving us stranded. We just sat there, because our artillery was doing a good job ahead of us, and we were almost out of ammunition. Meanwhile, infantry had crossed the river to reinforce the bridgehead and a counter-attack never materialized. When our engineers built another bridge to the South we were able to attack instead of being attacked."

March 30th found us embroiled in the attack on Mannheim, having crossed North of the city at Worms. There we were, again, coming from the North, when a day before we had been on the other side of the river to the South!

We had been assigned to General Patch's 7th Army a few days earlier. I believe that was the time I saw General Patton pull up in his command car. He was wearing his usual white-handled revolvers, breeches and Eisenhower jacket. Our crew happened to be staying in a German's house in Edenkoben, a few doors down from Division Headquarters at the time; since Combat Command "A" was taking the rear position for the next push.

When Patton came out, after only a couple of minutes, he was flanked by two sergeants, slightly to his rear. Before the command car moved out of sight the sergeants had spread the word, "We're moving out right away." When Gen. Patton said "move out" you didn't ask him when! One sergeant went up the street, the other went down. Our wire sergeant, Ellya, immediately assigned one man to go for rations, another to check gas and water, and the rest of us, to clean up the room where we had been sleeping. We rolled up our duffle a little tighter, then two of us cleaned up.

Ellya and Hap loaded our bags on the halftrack. After an inspector checked out our living quarters we walked quickly to the vehicles already lined up outside, ready to go. The inspector was on his way to the halftrack when I saw Frank putting the lid on the water can. "That's good timing," I said. Frank smiled "I had to leave it off until he came, because the water can is filled with wine." I stifled a laugh as the inspector came up and shined a flashlight into the 5-gallon water can, and the gas can on the other side. Hoby was up forward with Major Dan Hazen, the rest of us were in the halftrack. From the time Patton had given the word 'til the time we left was 15 minutes. More than ten thousand men were on their way! We were next to last to pull out.

Frank was humming a tune. He was always happy, especially so because he had put one over on the headquarters sergeant who inspected the hidden wine and found it to be water.

The rest of the division, below the 17,000 top strength, was situated in nearby towns. They all moved out at about the same time we did, proving that all our phone lines were in, and communications were up to Patton's standards of immediacy! I remember the look on the faces of the friendly Germans where we had stayed when we took the cover off the 50-caliber machine gun. They must have had relatives in the German Army.

I believe this was the town where we had the first real comfort days of the war. Even

Here's how we did it in World War II, and there is a good chance that the men you see piloting the DUKW are Navy men. The reel the wireman are rolling is cable. Two soldiers have managed to keep their carbines over their shoulders. They are tightening the cable, pulling against the current of the river, which in this case happens to be the Rhine. (U.S. Army Signal Corps Photo.)

though we had to sleep on the floor, the conditions were better than usual. We still had to run lines to all our battalions, but eating conditions were better. Breakfast brought us milk direct from the two cows in the back, lunch a bottle of wine from the basement stock, and dinner a short glass of schnapps to go with the hot meals we carried from just a block away.

In return, we all got together to help move a five foot high keg of cider up the cellar steps on a couple of bending boards. It took most of our crew to move this keg up the stairs and flip it onto a waiting cart. Away it went to market, pulled by a staunch farm horse.

Engineers of our 55th Armored Engineer Battalion had put the bridge across at Worms after the bridgehead had been established by the 63rd Division. We were slated to spearhead the 7th Army as it drove into Bavaria and Hitler's much-touted "stronghold." We caught up to the 63rd Infantry Division at Heidelberg, and were surprised to find that the city had surrendered by phone. It was easy to hook our lines directly into the switching terminal. In the future we found it easier to disconnect lines leading to the East, instead of cutting them as we had been doing.

SURRENDER BY PHONE
Our signal crews have quite a flair
For running wire wet or dry;
To tap in where the line is bare
They climb cement poles, way up high.

Or where rain or streams abound
A weasel lays the line around
Artillery or tank compound.

When Patton sends his armor through
We spin, like spiders, slender lines...
Communications to renew.
Incoming shells, and sometimes mines,
Get in our way so we rue
The day we took this road;
Until a call from Patton comes, to goad
Us toward the town ahead...
Where we can drop our switchboard load
And put our wire to bed;
Or connect with the enemy instead
To give them a chance to say
"We will surrender today."

I found out that General Patton didn't merely "throw" a division across the Rhine. He employed elements of the U.S. Navy, complete with landing craft! A friend of mine had asked one of the boat handlers (sort of like horse handlers in the cavalry) what unit he was with and he replied, proudly, "The Navy, sir," although my friend was a private at the time.

In earlier wars, signals were sent across rivers with Morse code or wire. In the above illustration, the shoulder-carried wire just wasn't making it.

6th Armored Division infantrymen are ferried across the Rhine near Nierstein, Germany by U.S. 3rd Army "Ducks" on the 25th of March, 1945. (Courtesy of Patton Library.)

This craft looks like it was made up from a jeep and 55-gallon drums. Shown in a training mode (notice the new army fatigue hats), the wire rack is made for the larger reels, but only a small reel is in use.

CHAPTER 10
END RUN WITH THE SEVENTH ARMY

Many vignettes were taking place at the various Rhine crossings. All up and down the river, our heavily armed P-47's were hunting the German tanks. Dave Eldridge, one of our pilots with the 406th Fighter Group explains how his plane could easily knock out an enemy tank: "Our armament consisted of eight fifty caliber wing-mounted machine guns. These guns were set to converge, with armor-piercing shells alternating with incendiary tracers. When this combination hit a tank, the tank would just explode. I'm sure gasoline stored outside the tank had something to do with this. We also carried two or three 500-lb. bombs, and later on six rockets were added to this arsenal."

Eldridge told of one incident that showed how our flyers looked after each other: "I was over enemy lines on the hunt for Gerry tanks when my engine was hit with a 20-mm anti-aircraft burst, and oil came spewing out to cover my windshield. I wasn't hurt but could not see a thing. Soon my attention was caught by one of our planes, close by on the left, wagging its wings to get my attention. James Shoene had elected to act as my wing man and lead me back to the base. I stayed even with him. I knew he was making a straight run for the home field when he went lower and lower. I still couldn't see out of the oil-slicked windshield, so I kept my eyes riveted on Jim. When he put his flaps down, I put mine down. Suddenly, he drew his finger across his throat, and with only a moment's hesitation I cut the engine and dropped onto the runway beside him, safe as a bird."

Eldridge was also involved in an episode that indicates how our ingenuity helped win the war. "Sometimes messages from the ground just weren't clear enough, so I volunteered for 'Operation Horsefly'...to help out in a L-5 liaison plane attached to a tank unit. We were relaying messages to the P-47's above, to tell them in language they would understand from up on high where to come in to bomb and strafe."

Meanwhile, farther North, Roy Colsey's main job as a Liaison Pilot was to spot the enemy artillery from his Piper Cub. Roy said, "Out of 160 Missions I was only hit once - got a small piece of shrapnel in my leg, and only a couple of holes in the fabric of the plane. We would find pieces of metal to sit on so we wouldn't get hit in the butt. It was mostly small arms fire we had to worry about because we flew so low. The larger ack-ack guns didn't aim for us because they didn't want to give away their position."

Roy spoke of another technique he used for spotting when he didn't know the exact azimuth. "Sometimes I had an observer with me, so it was easy for him to get a compass reading, and I could concentrate on flying the plane. When I was alone it was faster to say 'fire on me.' Of course I would tell them to fire beyond, maybe a half mile or more. The shells would arch overhead and explode near or on the enemy artillery, and I could easily re-direct to the right or left. There was always the thought that the shells would fall short and my plane would be in the way."

Roy breathed a sigh of relief when the war was over. Even though he liked to fly, and could have gotten a small plane license without a test, he confided that his desire to fly left him when he was discharged.

On the ground, we got used to the whistle of artillery shells and could tell the difference between outgoing and incoming shells. The saying was that if you heard the incoming shell you didn't have to worry about it. The distinctive outgoing sound didn't seem to bother us.

I can imagine that I would feel different up in a small liaison plane if I knew the artillery aimed at the enemy was going directly over my head and that I was responsible for the trajectory. It was one of those cases where your first mistake could be your last. Up a pole was as high as I wanted to get.

Our liaison planes did get shot at, though as many times as not they would be spared because the enemy did not want to give away their position. Only a couple were assigned to each division, so it was important to keep them running. We had units whose duty it was to repair them, such as the 43rd Mobile Repair and Reclamation, SQH. Men from this unit are shown assembling a metal wing structure for a Piper Cub. When the photo below was taken, the unit maintained a shop in Bettelaineville, France.

The Tenth crossed the Rhine, and was ready to pounce on Heidelberg a few days later. Heidelberg, red rose of the Neckar River. Somehow, the message came to us to spare the city, ancient seat of learning. Our tankers would have to find another city to ply their trade. The enemy wanted us to spare their city, and spare it we would. Many of the officers who opposed us had been trained in this city, but it was the mayor and the people of the city who capitulated. Other wicked battles would follow...railheads that were more significant to the Nazi war effort than they were to their educational and historical mindset.

We pressed on, as though in overdrive; in Third Army one day, Seventh Army the next. After March 23, we were definitely in the Seventh Army, having been exchanged for the Sixth Armored. It was like a General's chess game. We swung southeast toward Heilbronn with different divisions to help take the cities along the way. We would now be in close association with men of the 36th, 44th, 100th and 103rd Infantry Divisions along

Moving up with the front, a repair shop for mission planes remains close to the action(Courtesy of Patton Library, Oakes photo.)

the way. More of their infantry would be riding on our tanks. Our replacements had not caught up to us, so there was room on the tanks for some of their men. It was the early part of April.

The once-great German Army was existing on the wings of fear. Their phalanx of Tiger tanks was gone. Divisions facing us had only a few Tiger tanks left. We had learned to seek out these few lonely ravagers that were a magnet for our faster tanks. Some of our Shermans had been equipped with the new 90-mm cannons and were ready to hunt enemy tanks with a vengeance!

Lots of prisoners were taken, even without the persuading grenades. SS troops were different. They took longer to surrender. Dour-faced boys of fifteen or less had been trained to hate, but they learned to surrender. I remember once walking by mistake through a long hospital tent filled with SS troops. My ear had swelled up from a cold and the Army Doctor sent me to the rear because he thought it was a mastoid problem. I helped the healthier soldiers with some chores until the swelling went down, discovering the desire of men to want to return to their outfits.

I tried to be nonchalant when I walked through the tent full of about a hundred black-uniformed Nazi prisoners. The young teenagers emanated the most hatred as they gave me wicked stares. All I was doing was walking through the tent! Maybe I wasn't supposed to be there, but none of them took it as a humorous situation. I felt no hatred toward them, and showed none, yet received lots of scowls, and not a single smile. They must have been fed a pack of lies about us to hate that much!

It was understandable, then, to have so much opposition when we reached Heilbronn, an important rail center and hub for trains coming from the North. We were in the process of blocking any planned enemy retreat toward Bavaria. If Spring was in the air, it was also on the ground. Hitler's retreating troops had churned up the roads. Add to that recipe a couple hundred of our tanks and thousands of freed POW's and slave laborers moving the other way and you can imagine the mud. Fortunately, it didn't rain every day, so our tanks rolled right through the mud, and were able to out-maneuver the German tanks.

Our job was as tough as ever. The wire lay along the road as we unrolled it from our mounted A-frames. By the time we pulled it hand-over-hand it was rain-soaked and muddy. I remember one entire week my clothes were so wet the only place I could dry my hands was between my legs. Our jackets were soggy, and wool shirts were wet. A line of displaced persons in assorted old army uniforms trudged toward us, reaching to the horizon. Hoby and I were all alone, protected only by our jeep and carbines which we kept handy.

We had stopped at an intersection to check direction when a huge brown-uniformed man approached a pile of stacked rifles evidently taken from militia by our troops. He picked up a rifle about the size of an M1, but definitely older, while Hoby and I sat in the jeep, our attention riveted on him. "I guess there's no ammunition in those guns," Hoby observed. With that, the rugged-looking man smiled at us, and, in token, broke the rifle over his knee! "He looks to be in pretty good shape," I commented, as we breathed a collective sigh of relief. They walked on toward the rear, two and three abreast, headed for freedom. We continued to follow the wire to catch up with the rest of our crew.

Heilbronn proved too tough a nut for us to crack alone. It took the combined effort of our tanks and the 100th Infantry Division just to get a toe-hold in the city. The defenders were well fortified, so we were finally told to by-pass the city and let the 100th finish the job. We were still in a rush to cut down into Bavaria, now that some replacements had caught up with us.

By the time we reached Crailsheim the resistance seemed lighter, but in no time it became a pocket of trouble. Again, we were cut off from all sides. Supplies were not getting through. Joseph Radbill, from our 132nd Ordnance, told of having to send a two or three-tank convoy back to bring up parts. Now we couldn't even do that. Just when we thought it was getting easier to drive through!

I remember the German jets that came in out of the sun. After their first abortive run we watched as they missed the town by pulling up too soon. Our anti-aircraft guns also missed by quite a measure before the small planes vanished. After the first run, we stood out in the street to watch these small planes pull up too soon to hit anything.

It was soon time to exit Crailsheim when the 63rd Infantry Division arrived to take over. The Tenth shot across to the picture-postcard town of Oehringen, where we licked our wounds and prepared to go where we were least expected - South. So far, the

(U.S. Army Photo, Courtesy of Patton Library.)

German artillery had been bothersome. Shellbursts followed us to Oehringen, where we were bombarded off-and-on while awaiting supplies.

The Luftwaffe was less noticeable. Now they were working on the 63rd in Crailsheim. While we waited in Oehringen, Richard Bright, of our ordnance, must have repaired many machine guns, while his other buddies worked on the tanks.

When Oehringen was left far in our wake, our time-table had been stepped up again. Nightly stops were back to a town-a-night basis, while skipping several towns on the way. We were into April and days brought warmth, much like April days back in Pennsylvania. The weasels were working well out along streams and edges of farm pastures, although one of them hit a bouncing betty mine with its track, managing to miss the two wiremen inside.

The 63rd Infantry Division caught up to us again and helped us play river roulette. We went over so many rivers I lost count. Some, we captured the bridges, but most of them had to be crossed by our 55th Armored Engineers, using pontoons brought up by a flock of large trucks. If the rivers were large an additional engineer Battalion was assigned.

Slightly north, troops of Patton's Third Army uncovered gold bullion and art treasures, still stamped with names of cities from which they were stolen by the Nazis. The troops happened to get the information from a civilian. Generals Omar Bradley, George Patton, and Supreme Commander Dwight Eisenhower look at stolen art stashed deep in a salt mine. It was April 12, 1945; an important enough event to bring the generals together.

While we waited for our engineers to put a bridge across the Danube I got a chance to write a letter home. Here is an excerpt from that letter: "We get up at five tomorrow morning and so - to bed. The rest of the crew just got back from laying a line. They went out in the weasel. Corb boiled some rabbit the other night and it tasted darned good. Today when we pulled into this town a girl ran up with a Jerry field phone and plunked it down on Hank's trailer."

The night we boiled that rabbit may have been the night we also had rabbit stew,

(Courtesy of 103rd Divison.)   *(Courtesy of 42nd Divison.)*

Some rumors are being spread that the Holocaust was staged. Do these pictures looked staged? Study them. Study man's inhumanity to man and be ashamed if you were one of those who spread a rumor that it "didn't happen." Bill Wallace and the rest of the 42nd Division, attached to the 7th Army, fought into Dachau from the West in time to find stacks of people who hadn't been dead too long. "We counted 50 boxcars full of dead bodies," said Wallace. The 45th Division, attached to the 3rd Army, enterd Dachau on the same day, from the East. Jim Ortoleva's collection was given to him by a prisoner who took photos with a camera he stole from an S.S. guard. The three scenes, and some too dramatic to show, were seen by over 40,000 in the 103rd, 42nd, and 45th divisions. (Courtesy of Nerin Gun.)

reminding me of the Bill Mauldin cartoon of Willie and Joe where one of them cautions the other to be careful when he dropped the can of c-rations in the soup because there was a chicken stewing on the bottom. Our stew was also cooked in a helmet, which we were careful not to scorch, because we weren't supposed to use our helmets for cooking. When in the Third Army we couldn't dress like Willie and Joe, but in the Seventh Army, at least we could have a laugh at the cartoons.

STILL IN BATTLE
Yes, I'm still here
Perhaps for the nounce;
May be a year.
Oh yes, a nice jounce
T'would be to fear
Not the whine of a shell -
To have been told "You are
Delivered out of hell."

BEACHHEAD NEWS

This Newspaper Must Not Fall Into Enemy Hands

VOL. I, No. 282   Founded on Anzio . . . Printed in Germany   Tuesday, April 24, 1945

10th Armd, 44th Cross Danube

We went on down to the Danube River and across with 44th Division infantry riding on our 10th Armored tanks. It was April 22nd and we had received word that Patton had been made a full general on the 17th. The honor was late in coming because he mis-diagnosed a soldier's condition and tried to slap him back to reality. How fortunate for the Allies that this student of tank tactics was allowed to continue to lead!

One sunny day I was with the crew in the halftrack, looking for a way to bring the wire in from the next town, which our tanks had not yet taken. We had swung out into a field, headed for the town ahead. Suddenly we came upon the tanks. We could see them a mile away, hear the explosions and see the smoke emanating from the guns as our tank turrets swung toward the woods on the right. A Messerschmidt zoomed overhead from behind us, headed for the tanks up ahead. Sgt. Ellya voiced our thoughts when he said, "Let's get out of the field; I don't think they're ready for our wire up there."

We turned toward a woods on the left. The trees were close together, but a dirt road ran in the wrong direction,so we circled back toward the main road again. "Guess we'll have to climb poles all day, again," commented Hap with a smile. While we were still on the dirt road, a deer ran across in front of the track. Ellya jumped out on the right and let loose with his carbine before the deer had a chance for a second jump. We spent just a few minutes while Ellya supervised skinning of the deer. The rest of the day was routine, but we had deer meat for dinner, although a mite late, because we had to go on to the following town with our wire, and darkness had set in before we returned. It was good we had the deer meat because the hot food line had closed for the evening.

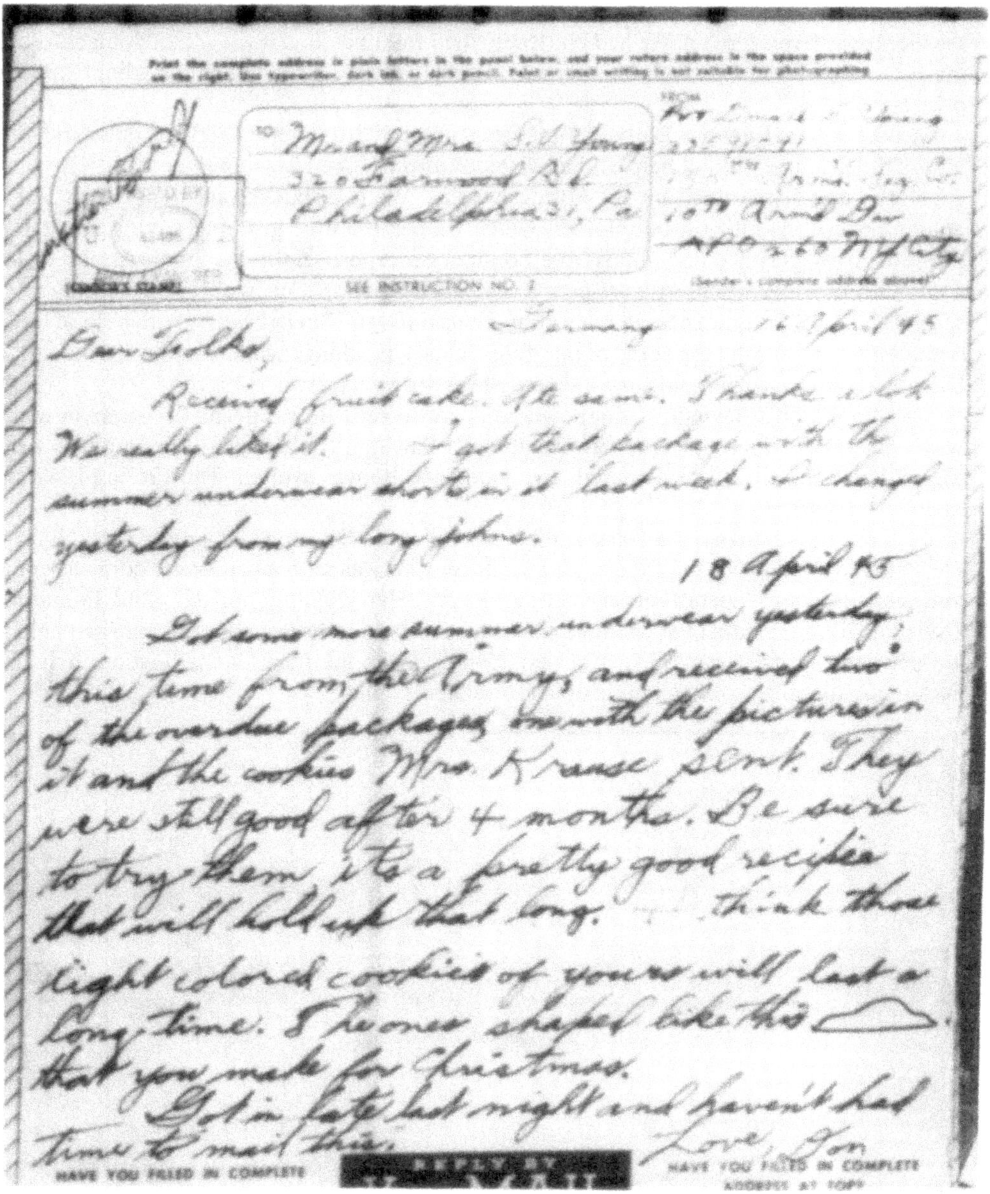

To: Mr. and Mrs. S. A. Young
320 Farmwood Rd.
Philadelphia 31, Pa.

From: Pvt. Smeal A. Young
[service number]
[unit]
10th Armd Div.
APO 260 N.Y. City

Germany   16 April 45

Dear Folks,

Received fruit cake. Ate same. Thanks a lot. We really liked it.   I got that package with the summer underwear shorts in it last week, & changed yesterday from my long johns.

                                   18 April 45

Got some more summer underwear yesterday, this time from the Army, and received two of the overdue packages, one with the pictures in it and the cookies Mrs. Krause sent. They were still good after 4 months. Be sure to try them it's a pretty good recipe that will hold up that long.   think those light colored cookies of yours will last a long time. The ones shaped like this ⌒. that you make for Christmas.

Got in late last night and haven't had time to mail this.

                                   Love, Son

While waiting for a bridge to be built over the Danube it was letter-writing time again. It was difficult to get paper to write on, but some of us had kept some V-mail in our duffle bags. This letter shows how the warmer weather was a change for the better.

Our tanks had swung around the town and surprised the enemy. Their road block was of no use and they had to withdraw, or be cut off completely.

The next large town was Ulm, somewhat South of Heilbronn, so it was difficult for the Germans to reinforce it. We had bottled up their rail lines, and it wasn't too long before the 10th Armored and the 44th Infantry had taken the town, and, along with it, about 2,000 prisoners.

Like our 55th Engineer Battalion, engineers of the 103rd Infantry Division put a bridge across the Danube without help of the twisted timbers of the blown bridge.

Hoby and I were glad for the Spring weather. We had shucked our long johns and gotten most of the mud off our clothes, which were still a little grungy. Moving fast, the Seventh Army was heading almost due South at times, especially the Tenth Armored. I couldn't remember when we were ever a reserve division. Seems we went from one hot spot to another. The quickness of our armor got us through Ulm in a hurry, with help of the 44th. We swung southwest, some of our division moving along the bank of the formidable Danube river to Ehingen on April 23. A day later we were across the river.

Again, Patch's Seventh Army powered down toward Bavaria. The divisions in our way had been reduced to stubborn roadblocks, but don't tell that to our infantry. At Memmingen the enemy surrendered, and another battle was averted. The circling P-47's may have contributed!

On our move toward the Danube the 42nd Rainbow Division was on our flank, with the Third Army just North of them. Bill Wallace, who was with an anti-tank company of nine guns told of General Patton visiting General Harry Collins, of the 42nd Infantry Division. "Patton came over on more than one occasion to borrow our company to help with one of his spearheads. Since our company was on the flank of the Seventh Army, Patton could easily work us into his plans," related Wallace.

(Photo is by the 103rd Signal Company.)

Our 10th Armored also had multiple rocket launchers. The contraption attached to this 10th Armored tank attests to the fact that we also could produce the swoosh that became a frightening sound to the enemy. This photo was taken earlier, in March, when our troops were with the 3rd Army near Losheim, Germany. (Courtesy of Patton Library.)

Wallace's company of nine guns and 90 men was three times as large as the usual anti-tank unit. You can bet this is the one Patton would pick! He could swing these guns to the side of the road at night more quietly than the lumbering tanks that would usually have to back into position until time to attack. Each gun had a ten-man support team, which was especially effective if the parent division was short of infantry. The team included an air-cooled 30-caliber machine gun, B.A.R., bazooka, six M-1 rifles, and the sergeant had a carbine.

The surrender of Memmingen brought 3,936 Allied prisoners to freedom: 506 American, 772 British, 414 French, and 625 Russian.

A couple of warm days were on the way. "No more long johns!" shouted Frank with a relish. Fields were drying out with the merciful sun. It was easier going. Sporadic shelling had decent intervals in between the bursts, so the event was over before our surge of fear. Nervous laughter abounded. Wire dragging in the ditch threw up plumes of dust when we flipped it to the side. We were able to tap in to the German wire to save a few reels of our own because the artillery had not softened up the roads as much as usual. We moved too fast. The enemy retreated.

Tankers had less opposition, and were more comfortable in their tanks. They didn't freeze! However, on hot days they marinated in their own perspiration. Sometimes it wasn't the sun that made them sweat. Our men were still getting shot. At this point in the war, enemy troops who weren't shooting or dying were surrendering. They were coming forward in groups, with one of them carrying a white flag on a stick. It looked like they were using bedsheets or large towels. It must have been hard for them to find enough white material. Germans were giving up by the thousands, finally ignoring their officers orders to fight to the last man. They had tasted defeat for months and were willing to give up to us before their unit might be sent to the Russian front. The Russians, who had been invaded, didn't like to take prisoners. They would, but they didn't like it. German officers were deserting their men. We found a batch of them down in Bavaria later on.

We climbed poles all day from dawn to dusk, but considered ourselves fortunate to be, most of the time, one to three miles from the front. We had days when artillery was aimed at our halftrack or jeep. Most of the time the enemy guns were aiming for our tank concentrations or artillery when their spotter planes could find them. We must have been secondary targets, but they wasted a few shells on us anyway. They were the kind of instances that burn into your memory, depending on how close the explosion came.

At Memmingen we turned due West and derisively ran over the opposition. We had crossed the Iller without breaking stride, but the Lech river was another story. It was full from Spring run-off. Facing opposition and a blown bridge at Landsberg, our troops scooted South again to effect another surprise crossing 24 miles further down at Schongau.

Our tanks ran down through narrow valleys between the mountains. Several people told us they had never seen tanks down here...which didn't mean there wasn't any resistance! It was easy for the enemy troops to set up roadblocks. One town we came upon had just been hit by our tanks and infantry in time to prevent a German troop train from either arriving intact or retreating in time. The train was burning. Packs and equipment were strewn about, but the dead and wounded had already been removed.

Just as we were getting used to a little better weather, we climbed higher up the pass into what I think was the last blizzard in our sector. Swirling winds buffeted us as we strung wire over intersections along the way. In between we tapped into roadside lines; open wire at the top of 30-ft. high cement poles. It was cold going again, but was over soon.

There was one of these cement poles, at least 30 ft. high, that I climbed up to connect our line and follow the two wires to the next town. I couldn't see either end hanging down, and the wire was about an eighth of an inch thick, indicating a hot wire. I hesitated. "Cut it on this side," yelled Sgt. Ellya. "Isn't it hot?" I retorted. "Cut it!" the whole crew shouted, so I gingerly tapped it with my pliers, then proceeded to cut the wire. I held my breath, although that wouldn't have done me any good if the wire was hot. Maybe the wire wasn't hot, but I was sweating a little, while the crew broke up laughing. They knew the wires were dead. We spliced on our wire and followed the road, keeping the tall towers in view while a couple of exercise miles were saved.

We were starting to see brightly painted murals on some of the chalet-style buildings along the way. Part of our division headed for Garmish through Oberammergau, world-known for its Passion Play. The rest of us swung South in a pincer movement that put us in a position to take the twin Bavarian towns of Garmish-Partenkirchen.

One stretch of back-road towns exhibited rows of old slanted poles with wire hanging down, laced with shrapnel holes. Climbing up the high side of one of these, my hook hit an opening and I was barely able to hang on. As I ended up on the low side of the pole I had to come all the way down and start up again, on the high side. It wouldn't do to break my neck now that we had the enemy on the run. That situation wasn't as dangerous as what happened to one of our men. I forget who was up the pole, but it was a sergeant or one of the men who had a lot of climbing experience. Several of us were standing around at the bottom of this pole waiting for him to splice a line, or tie it on, when suddenly a shot rang out and a sharp whistle as the bullet passed overhead. He actually ran down the pole. We all grabbed our carbines and looked up the hill for the sniper, but he was gone over the crest. "That was quite an exhibit of pole running; do it again in case someone missed it," said Hap with his dry sense of humor.

So it went, on down into Bavaria. I remember carrying five lines on my shoulder to tie all five diagonally over an intersection. A thought came to mind how our mind and bodies adapt to a whole new line of work.

We see more civilians down here than we have, which attests to the speed at which our division has been moving. The people may not have been brainwashed as much, and seem to take no special pains to hide. We see women carrying heavy loads on their way to market, and in the fields pounding stakes to anchor their cattle. Maybe that's to keep cows from wandering off where they might end up in a G.I stew.

It was a dark night when we met another of our crews, looking for the same break in the line, which ran along a fence. "It must be around here somewhere...we didn't find it coming from our direction," Hap disclosed. The four of us sloshed around in the mud, tapping in on a bunch of lines with our field phones, getting our switchboard in one direction and theirs in the other. We didn't mind a little mud with Spring on the way. I tapped into a line closer to where they were standing, with Hoby masking the light from his flashlight. Suddenly, the pin went into the second strand of the wire and I felt an unmistakable jolt! I had tapped into a 220-volt line one of our units had run from a captured German generator. There was muffled laughter, because we didn't want our troops to come out of the blacked-out house with their guns blazing. I was trained to hold 110 volts and let the current go through my body - but not 220! And certainly not when standing in the mud with wet feet.

It took us about 20 minutes to find the field phone. It was tan, and the mud was tan, and I must have thrown it to get away from the charge. We kept as quiet as possible so the other unit wouldn't come out shooting. The outline of light around their blacked-out windows was barely visible. "Well, someone is comfortable tonight," said Frank. We finally found the break in our wire and fixed it...our last duty that day.

When we were going on down through the Black Forest Hoby and I had the privilege of shooting trouble on lines another crew had stretched out for miles through thick pine trees on either side of the road. It was necessary to go back into the woods for 10 or 15 feet to find the line. It looked like they had pulled it through by hand, though in some places we could see jeep tracks where the pine needles were thinner. We moved the jeep several times and trudged together through the deep woods.Finally we narrowed down the area of the break by checking back and forth, and were in the process of following the line through the late afternoon shadows. Hoby was in the lead, when he stopped quickly and stooped down. "Don, it's been cut!"

At that moment, we didn't stop to fix the wire. We both ran back to the jeep, about 40 feet away (though it seemed like 100 feet) and got our carbines, then went back to fix the line, keeping an eye out for a sniper, who was long gone. We were supposed to have our carbines on hand at all times. I even carried mine into a church one time, and felt very awkward when it banged against the pew. At the time, there was no place to leave it. Wiremen should have sidearms.

Through the mountain passes we went...prongs of armor led by our fast recon tanks. We could accomplish now, with 50% of our mobile infantry, what a month ago we had trouble doing with a full compliment of troops - that is, blasting through opposition at break-neck speed. At the height of battle, reinforcements were coming up regularly. Now, they were scarce. But opposition was scarce. Raw German recruits were surrendering by the thousands. Old timers, back from German hospitals, were also giving up; glad to have an excuse to surrender to the Americans. One of these soldiers who later helped pick up wire as a prisoner of war told how he was glad to be sent to this part of the line. He had fought the Russians with their massed artillery and heavy tanks that took on the Germans head-on, coming at them in wave after wave.

The United States had produced 60,973 tanks of all kinds; Britain, 23,202, and the U.S.S.R. 54,500. Compare with these figures the tank production of the Axis powers: 19,926 for Germany, 4,600 for Italy and 2,464 for Japan. We had stopped the last German pincer movement at the Bulge around Bastogne, and were winding down the last large tank battles. Gone was the incessant whine of the 88's, the woosh of the 105's and the yodeling wobble of the multiple rockets that we came to know toward the end of the conflict.

North of us, Patton's Third Army moved quickly toward Berlin. Later, we found out he was commanded to go slower and give the Russians time to get there. There were so many Germans surrendering to the Third Army it was impeding their progress somewhat. The Russian front had been stripped of some good German troops for the Bulge effort, but new men were being sent to the Russian front.

Rolf Donath, who worked through the ranks from private to lieutenant in the German infantry was one of those rushed up to Leningrad as a replacement. "We were put on an old cattle train with open cars," related Rolf. "The engine pushed a car loaded with rocks ahead of it to protect the engine, and us, from any explosions. It did just that when we hit a mine, and partisans shot with machine guns from ambush, so it took us a while to get through to Russia. We got there just before our German troops became surrounded...just in time to help them break out, heading back toward Germany.

"We went in with 150 men and came out with 25. I was wounded when a mortar exploded in the trees and I got several pieces of shrapnel in my left shoulder. When I got back to the front again I was 18 and already an experienced soldier. We were still on the defense. A new Field Marshall had been assigned to our outfit. He was a real Nazi and had some officers shot just to maintain discipline! A couple of times I helped run wire to our command headquarters. Our infantry wiremen had a backpack with a wire reel on it. I could run pretty fast, and didn't get hit.

"Just East of Berlin I got hit again with machine gun fire and walked 15 kilometers to the first aid station. While recuperating, I got a field commission as lieutenant; was sent back for training and got a pass to see my mother and dad. My experience as an officer lasted three days before I was wounded for the third time. Soon after, the war ended. Of thirty men from my home town, only three of us returned."

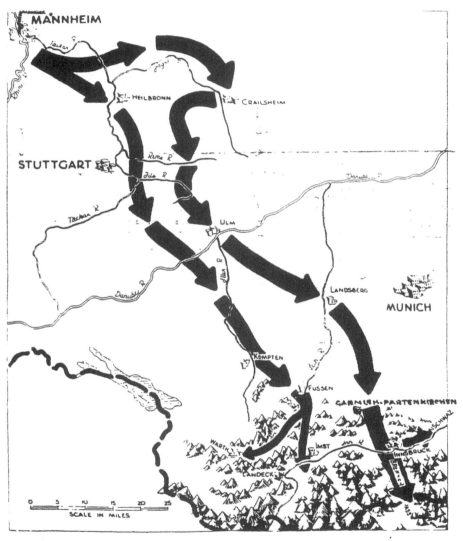

This map from the Beachhead News of May 20, 1945, shows the 7th Army route during the last European phase of World War II. The 10th Armored fought into Garmish-Partenkirchen, and ranged out from there as far as Insbruck and the Austrian border. The fighting officially ended on May 9, 1945 while we were in Garmish.

The Modern Abrams Tank.
(Photo courtesy of Patton Museum.)

CHAPTER 11
ON TO GARMISH-PARTENKIRCHEN

In one case, down toward the Bavarian sector, our men had defeated the opposing division, chasing them on down the road. However, we met extended civilian resistance: Nazi youth, possibly German soldiers reverting to civilian dress - certainly harmful to our infantry. We made sure this wouldn't happen again to jeopardize our soldiers. Our excellent communications helped organize a count-down to effect a simultaneous barrage. Not just artillery! Tanks, tank destroyers, mortars...caused a rumble that lasted for a long echo. I think a bombing raid was also called for the same time frame, to complete destruction of the town. The next day I passed the village, which indeed from a mile away looked like it was pretty well demolished. This may have been the last vestige of civilian cooperation with the Hitler regime.

One of the rules of war is that civilians have to remain neutral or they will be treated as soldiers. The enemy used this rule to invade and subjugate whole countries to their will, claiming they were at war.

All along the way, except at Heidelberg, where surrender was by phone, and Trier, where we captured one, bridges had been destroyed by retreating troops so our engineer battalions had to build temporary ones. However, as we came down into Bavaria the highest bridge was kept intact by the local people who knew that the stream way below was fordable...and it might be a long time before they would get another bridge to connect their mountain-side roads.

You would think that Hitler would have built heavy fortifications in these mountains, which could have been easy to defend; but he must not have expected so quick a penetration, especially by armor! Some people told us, to their knowledge, tanks had never been down in this area. Hitler probably felt that his mountain retreat was safe. It is thought that there would be more opposition down toward Bavaria, but it looks like Patton's Third Army moved too fast for any big exodus into this sector. We were now in General Patch's Seventh Army. By this move, our division loses a little of its identity in History. When someone is researching the Third Army, we disappear. Researchers can't keep tabs on us, any more than the Germans could! That's why it is important to set the record straight, to emphasize the contributions of the Tenth Armored, the necessity for proper use of armor as suggested by Patton, and the possibility to inject into tactical thinking the idea of fluidity and speed, which may only be in the vocabulary of some "tank" generals still in Washington. Thank God for good battlefield generals! May they not all retire.

However, we begin to hope that wars will be small, and far between:

PEACE
Peace is here again.
A touch of it comes, 'neath
Nature's spell - a wren
Perched on a low branch; a wreath
Of pine boughs framing
The bird 'gainst golden sky.
But as, day waning,
Sunset's beauty rests my
Mind, I think of things

Remote from guns and tanks
And as the wren sings
I relax, and give thanks
To God who released me
From anguish, and with
Nature's soothing key
My mental ban dismissed.
Once again I am myself.

Finally, we arrived in Garmish-Partenkirchen, end of the war for our division. Part of the Tenth Armored stayed in Oberammergau, home of the Passion Play. Houses in both towns were adorned with hand-painted scenes. Colorful designs wrapped around windows and arched doorways. Cows, returning from mountain pastures, were ushered down the main streets.

Mountains wrapped around the town, with the snow-capped Zugspitz in full view. The 150th Armored Signal Company was billeted in a row of homes with balconies shaded by roof overhangs. We slept in an end room on the floor, but we didn't mind, because it was also an end to our wandering.

There happened to be enough time off in the afternoon for me to keep in pole-climbing shape by jogging around the famous track outside town where G.I.'s trained. It was here athletes once prepared for the first Summer olympics held in Berlin a decade earlier on May 25, 1935, and at Garmish the following Winter. Jesse Owens, from Decatur, Alabama, and Ohio State University won the 100 and 200-meter dash and the broad jump. Ben Ogden, of Temple University was his coach.

In August, while I was on my way home, a track meet was held at Nurnberg. Thou-

Even today, cows walk down the main streets of Garmish.

sands of German prisoners worked to put the stadium in shape for G.I. track and field events. The meet attracted entries from all over the European Theatre.

It was fitting that Lt. John P. Hemcher, U.S. Army, Armored Infantry, was picked to escort General Patton to his seat at the meet. Hemcher had fought with two tank outfits in Bastogne. This must have been a big day for General Patton, as it certainly was for Lt. Hemcher, who was truly Officer of the Day. In 1912, Patton had placed fifth in the Olympic Pentathlon. Lt. Hemcher had received a battlefield commission. General Patton had just received his fourth star. In World War I he commanded a tank brigade.

"Everything went as planned," said Lt. Hemcher. "I met General Patton on the outskirts of Nurnberg. I saluted. In return he gave me one. I positioned troops at various intersections to protect the general and we went together to the stadium, along with 80,000 cheering G.I.'s.

"Patton suddenly started yelling and I wondered if maybe I had done something

Patton at the track meet. (By Hemcher.)

wrong, but couldn't think of anything. A group of Air Corps officers were sitting nearby. They looked very irritated, but didn't say a word. Patton was telling them to leave because they were out of uniform. They had taken wire supports out of their dress hats, which gave them a floppy look. Some of them were colonels. Nevertheless, they left in a hurry."

You may notice that the general is wearing his four stars, but not his white-handled revolvers. When he pinned the distinguished service cross on General McAuliffe after the Battle of the Bulge he wore the revolvers, but now, in peacetime, he was wearing his dress uniform, which didn't lend itself to the bulky revolvers he wore in combat. Maybe someone had cast aspersions at his special sidearms, although Patton scarcely needed an excuse to yell at someone who was out of uniform! After all, generals were permitted to wear side arms of their choosing.

Of course, there were not as many photos taken of General Patton in the battle garb after he received his four stars. At the track meet he was protected by the Officer of the Day, Lt. Hemcher, and his 50 men, some of whom were assigned to also guard intersections.

The only danger now was the night that marked the war's end, May 7, 1945. So many machine-gun tracers lit the sky, it was possible to get struck with a falling bullet. Don't know that anybody got hit, but I remembered the preceding Winter, watching a foot-long shell fragment as it bounced off a phone pole and fell clanging to the ground, still steaming. I suddenly had a thought I had been putting aside - "Maybe this time there's one with my name on it" - so I decided to stay inside.

Our signal company was holed up in Garmish for a month, ranging out for miles to pick up wire. A chalet-style building served as barracks for our crew. We could look out on grassy slopes of the surrounding hills, where sun-bathing women dotted the fields until about three in the afternoon.

Unfortunately, we were kept busy 'til then. If we weren't picking up wire we pulled guard duty or took turns at K.P. Including the wire crews of other divisions, we had abandoned 300,000 wire reels along the roads of our advances, some of which we now tried to find.

I managed to finagle a pass to go skiing on the Zugspitz, a towering peak we could see from Garmish. A cog railway took me up, clanking through the mountain, to emerge beneath the ski lodge. After the process of renting skis boots and poles it was time for a half-day of skiing. By the time I had travelled, the corn snow of a morning in May had turned wet. Skiers were attempting to wend their way down the slope, but ended up having to herringbone up again.

Normally, a two mile run could be made! Although May isn't the best month to ski, the wet snow on the Zugspitz was a lot like I was used to around Philadelphia,

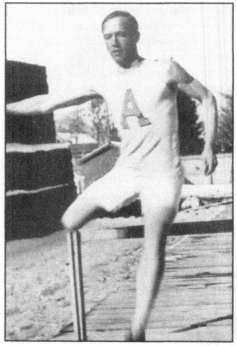

At age 27, Patton practices for the 1912 Olympics. (Courtesy of Patton Library.)

where the Buck Ridge Ski Club maintained a rope tow at Paxon Hollow Golf Club. So much for reminiscences as I climbed to the top of a rise, overlooking an unfenced drop-off to the valley below.

You will agree that dictators always underestimate the resolve of free men to fight for what is right - to eliminate oppression, if not at its inception, then later, in finality! There was no better proof of this than our march through Germany in World War II. The Tenth Armored Division suffered about 4,000 casualties out of a 17,000-man division augmented by many combat replacements. The casualties were mainly from our armored infantry and tank battalions. Engineers were casualties at river crossings.

Toward the end of the war, many of the thousands of German prisoners had learned by the grapevine that though we were tough, we were fair, and they surrendered. Others, their divisions down to a third of their size, gave up because our onslaught was as forceful as ever. We still fought with the fervor of free men, not with the pomposity of conquerors. By this time, many of the enemy had begun to realize that they had been ingrained with the wrong philosophy. They became weaker, wondering if they were ordered to fight to the end because there was still a chance of winning, or just for Hitler's insanity.

We fought to "get it done." Still happy-go-lucky, we were feared for the power unleashed by an armored division. The enemy also feared us for the lies of their leaders, who admonished them to fight to the last man. Then their officers withdrew to warmer climes. We found them by the dozens, rounded up in Bavaria by our riflemen and the infantry of accompanying divisions. The officers were ram-rod stiff even in surrender. They probably knew, more-so than their men, that they would be treated well.

These German Generals and Colonels were fierce in their adherence to duty and stubborn in their initial refusal to surrender, but in the end, left their troops to hold the bag.

The war ended in time for us to avert an atomic bomb attack by the Germans, who were closer to obtaining a production model than we were. Our troops also captured VII sites and stopped that threat.

When the infamous S.S. leader, young General Peiper, was caught it put an end to slaughter of Allied soldiers who had been captured. But not in time to prevent the deaths of most of 140 G.I.'s who were gunned down as they stood in a group, in the snow, during the first days of the "bulge" beyond Bastogne. In trying to "get ahead" by these acts of cruelty, the Nazi general ended up at the Nurnberg trials. He got 10-to-15 years, but served less time and ended up at his home several years later. He died when persons unknown fire-bombed his house. This is the way of cruel men - they somehow reach a fate similar to what they have meted out.

We had some new weapons of our own that were just coming into use. A secret 90-ton tank hit the testing stage. It was designed to roll over or through obstructions like the Siegfried Line. A double set of tracks, a low profile and slanted sides gave it an invincible appearance. However, it was 10 tons heavier than the German Tiger Tank, which may have proved a problem. The second set of tracks could be removed for shipping, which proved that the designers were aware of the weight, 95 tons when loaded! Only two were produced. One is located at Aberdeen, Maryland; the other at Fort Knox, Kentucky. Anyway, it shows that we tried to come up with a better and more formidable tank right away, but the war ended.

John Hemcher, who had three smaller tanks shot out from under him, was trained in this 4-man tank, and later went on to get a battlefield commission as lieutenant.

New weapons were in the works for our wire crews. One, a bazooka that would shoot wire over a river or across a field; another, a mortar that can shoot wire over a river or forest.

The 90mm tank gun, so effective at the end of the war, made way for the 105. In WW II the 105 was an artillery piece that could be towed easily and set up to rotate 360 degrees. It was also in use as a self-propelled artillery unit complete with tank treads. When the enemy attacked, the howitzer could be quickly moved.

A tank flame-thrower was often the best way to knock out a pillbox, especially in the islands, so this weapon is bound to last...maybe even be improved upon! Another weapon you don't hear much about is the ray gun. There has to be a breakthrough with this throwback to Buck Rogers! But now they call it a laser.

The new MIAZ Abrams tank weighs 69.54 tons. With four speeds forward, two in reverse, it can go 42 miles per hour...30mph cross country. Weapons include two 7.62 M240 machine guns and a 50-caliber; and sports a 120 mm cannon.

Among the host of significant features on this modern tank the newest include an Intervehicular Information System, Digital Communication, Position Navigation System, Single Channel Ground/Air Radio System, and Commander's Integrated Display.

These tank features were shown to me by John Purdy, director of the Patton Museum at Fort Knox, in answer to my question, "What's new in communication in recent years?" The answer to this seemed to sum up the years of Patton's work with tanks, to somehow get battle information to them. Purdy called it "INFORMATION TECHNOLOGY, carried over into Army operations, including tanks." At this point Purdy made clear, as Patton would say "Don't tell people how to do it, just tell them what to do".

"An integrated display allows maps and pictures of the entire battlefield to be sent to

Embellishments of Garmish buildings are more fanciful than ever.

a tank commander," Purdy disclosed. "The information comes out in a short burst, so the data can be captured by the tank commander without fear of it being stolen by someone trying to tune in on the frequency. With cell-phone network and its corresponding towers, we may have reduced the need for wire." What makes it feasible is that the "burst" of information can be aimed at the tank.

The solid sending disks have already been battle tested, and dents in the surface, from machine gun fire, do not seem to interfere with messages. Just as with wire, if you have enough towers in the right places, it works like a charm!

Mainstay WWII weapons were the 88 and thicker armor on Germany's side, better sights and mobility on ours. Our turrets turned faster and our tanks moved two to three times as fast as the bigger German tanks. And we had the production capacity, backed up by our Navy and supply capabilities.

We think our communications had an important part to play in helping us win the war, and it looks like they are better now.

The Tenth Armored broke up slowly, as company clerks tried to get the men with the most points home for Christmas, 1945. I was surprised to have 115 points, and soon found myself on a train bound for France.

Actually it was a bunch of boxcars with triple-tier bunks; attached to an engine. The dining car was just another boxcar, where we filed through to pick up a hot meal, then back again to wash the aluminum kits in five-gallon drums; one with soap for the initial wash; two with clear scalding water for a dip-and-swish rinse. Occasionally the train stopped on a siding to let another train go by, but we had to stay on during these stops.

Rest stops were far between, usually on the outskirts of a town where only bombed-out buildings bore witness to the engineer's impatience. When the train whistle blew you could see men running for their respective cars, pulling up their pants as they ran. Sometimes they had to settle for the wrong car, with willing hands reaching out to help them aboard as the train gradually gathered speed. Often, we had to wait on a siding as an express passed. Skeletons of towns flashed by, some with only the hallowed church spire still standing.

We finally reached the embarkation port of LeHarve, where hundreds of men found their trip home bogged down in a sea of paperwork. Because I could type, I took a chance and volunteered to help with the papers, along with dozens of company clerks. This time I had truly volunteered for typing! We worked for two straight days 'til about 10 P.M. with hope that whatever ship was in the harbor would wait for us.

After traveling orders were completed for our group of men from several divisions, assignment was made for us to leave on the next available ship headed for New York...for a passing acquaintance with the Grand Old Lady.

OUR LAST HURRAH...

HEADQUARTERS
150TH ARMORED SIGNAL COMPANY
TENTH ARMORED DIVISION
APO 260

4 June 1945.

SUBJECT: After Action Report. (10-30 May 1945).

TO: Commanding General, 10th Armored Division,
APO 260.

ATTENTION: G-3, I & E.

The unit has remained at Garmisch and through the entire period has been devoted to training a liminted amount on subjects specified by division. The large percentage of men in the unit have been occupied with wire work. The commercial switchboard was taken over and put into operation, first, manually and later automatic. In addition to that cables were spliced with the assistance of regular German employees in order to have telephone communication to all outlying units.

Radio Maintenance has checked all division radios. In this manner they were able to correct minor deficiencies as well as direct other sets be brought in for further repair.

Signal Supply has located German signal equipment and turned it into army depots.

Radio stations have been sending code on a predetermined frequency to stations in the division who care to copy for practice. The radio school continues to train operators and is contemplating a new class.

27

RICHARD W. FUCHS,
Capt, Sig C,
Comdg.

CLASSIFICATION
CANCELLED
BY AUTHORITY OF THE ADJUTANT GENERAL
DOWNGRADING COMMITTEE

90-ton T-28 had a crew of four and sported a 105mm cannon.

125

CHAPTER 12
HOME AGAIN

Soldiers waited up all night to see the Statue of Liberty. It loomed larger than we expected in the mist of morning, stirring thoughts akin to those experienced by early travelers who knew they were safe when it came into view.

What type of man would stay up all night to see the Statue of Liberty? Saviors of the peace, that's who! They came, they saw, they wondered about their future...what would tomorrow bring? They had turned back the tides of oppression. Sobered somewhat by loss in battle of new-found friends, the troops came home. Some, wounded several times, wanted to return to their outfit again and again. Now, they returned home.

Our group straggled lightheartedly down to a waiting train which whisked us to nearby Fort Hancock, New Jersey; hopefully, for mustering out! But it didn't work out that way. Instead, it appeared to be a center for mustering-in. Trained personnel sergeants talked with us on a one-on-one basis, asking whether we would like a 3-year or 6-year enlistment. There were many takers, but I didn't bite.

DREAM OF DISCHARGE
The new moon's bleak unwinking eye
Looks down upon this fort tonight.
All guns in hidden slumber lie
In token of potential might.

The harbor lights are on again,
And barracks at Fort Hancock too
Are live with light and men still sane
With hopes that soon they will be thru -

Discharged today, free as a lark.
This hopeful thought is always there.
I hear it now when night is dark;
I hear it in the rushing air...

The slash of surf and wind's wild whish
That seem to talk to me and say,
"My friend, you may have one more wish -
Yes, you will be discharged SOME DAY."

While we waited, the Army found many useful things for us to do. Fortunately, I got an assignment other than K.P. or guard duty. My typing ability landed me in prison. You must believe it was not by choice, but it worked out to be better than it sounds. The office in a nearby prison was staffed with guys and gals, most of them civilians.

The maximum security complex had walls 30 feet in height, and about that same number below ground, to prevent tunnels from being dug with serving spoons and other apparatus. It was interesting to be admitted through the large gates each morning on my way to work in the large prison office. (Yes, I got to go back to the base each evening!) Walking down the long corridor to the office was an experience in itself. It seemed that prisoners who said hello and stayed beside me for the five-minute walk would always have a story to relate, invariably one of wrongful imprisonment. One or two of the dozen or more "not guilty" explanations seemed plausible, although it was difficult to determine which of them could possibly be true.

One day I asked our office favorite, Helen, where I could get a haircut, and found out that they had a barber shop in the prison. This sounded interesting, and certainly became so when I ended up in the barber's chair, with a restricting striped barber's cape tied around my neck. "Cut it all off?" he asked, in what I hoped was a joking manner. "Just trim it a little," I replied, remembering to add "please." Actually, it was a good haircut, complete with a razor job on the neck hairs, also delivered with a remark or two!

The way out at day's end was even more difficult than getting in early in the morning. I.D.'s were checked, and passes looked at with scrutiny. I always made the bus back to base without incident. Any negative thoughts garnered during the day were dispersed by thoughts of getting home by Thanksgiving...or Christmas. It was also appropriate to use the technique of leaving all negative thoughts in the prison.

Except when we were with Patton, it was the old Army story again: hurry up and wait. For some reason I was boxcar-bound right past home town Philadelphia, back to Camp Gordon, Georgia...although the outfit in camp was no longer the Tenth Armored. It was the 95th. I wrote home that the 95th is moving out, but in retrospect, most of us were just waiting to be discharged.

However, it was only September 25, 1945. Most of this unit had been on passes to New Orleans, whiling away the days before discharge. It behooved me to do the same, thus avoiding K.P. and guard duty for a weekend. It was called a "three-day pass" the longest we could get. Unless, of course, a furlough could be obtained; in that case it would be 30 days. Most of the G.I.s held out for discharges. A furlough would only be a last-ditch attempt to get home for a holiday, but it looked like that was what we would have to take.

The shadows in New Orleans on a sunny day were made for memories. Wrought-iron gates and fences cast interesting patterns as I walked around Jackson Square...walking quickly through the tombstones (just to get to the tour ship on time). This was more up-beat. In fact, a dance band was on board, with sailors, soldiers, WACS and civilians all in attendance. I danced with a Red Cross girl on a pass without her uniform. The blues music was new to me, but it was conducive to the slow movement we were both used to. Before the war I had danced to the Glenn Miller orchestra at Steel Pier in Atlantic City, and to another big band at Sunnybrook Ballroom near Pottstown, Pennsylvania. It was the start of the Big Band Era. This night, in New Orleans, it seemed like the jazz of the big bands originated here.

We got along so well that Jean and I left the ship together as night arrived, and had dinner at the Blue Room of Hotel Roosevelt. I only remember what the meal cost because my letter home noted the amount - $8.50 for two. And that included a floor show!

Next, we strolled toward Basin Street, where the beat of true blues emanated from small bars with vine-draped outdoor terraces. Colored lights were placed strategically, so that the colors blended in with the shadows to lend an atmosphere of romance.

At one of these flagstone side yards a blues trio played, throbbing the sound of New Orleans music, so we went in and danced again. As the sun in New Orleans is sinking from sight, and the lamps on the side streets go on; then the music gets thicker and lasts all the night, with the laughter and dancing and song. And we find that the New Orleans rhythm is here with a beat that is solid and sweet. Then exotic romance is conveyed to the ear, causing dancers to shuffle their feet with a fervor kept dormant 'til music like this gives a feeling to all who are there of tranquility causing contentment and bliss - with soft music enchanting the air. And the moon o'er the rooftops exhibits her charms, shining down on the terrace so bright. We are dancing embraced in each other's arms - content for the rest of the night.

The music stayed at the same pace, rising and falling at the whim of the musicians: sax, base and drum set complete with washboard. As it rose and fell it would hit the same pulsing note, New Orleans style. This was romance, not war.

Discharge was interrupted by a furlough, during which I hitchhiked 600 miles home. The Army may have wanted me to use up my vacation time instead of having to pay me. I did get out before Christmas, on December 17, 1945. General Patton's jeep was involved in an accident and he died of a broken neck on December 21.

What had been an all-encompassing event in the life of our country had come to a close. Patton, designer of modern fast-moving armored divisions had saved many American lives by building into these divisions the ability to keep moving with relentless pressure. It was, indeed, the end of an era.

PATTON'S LAST DAYS

When all our troops led freedom home
To those who thought they were alone;
Then Patton came and led his men
To battle, never just to send
Them out into the bursting shells,
With rotting cows and carcass smells
That blend with smoke and noise of fire...
To aim at infantry and wire.

Yes, Patton was the kind of fellow
Who led beyond headquarter's cellar
Where lesser men thought danger near
But where they stayed they couldn't hear
The burst of bomb and blast of gun
That meant the Krauts were on the run;
The sound that Patton revelled in
When his Third Army men would win.
And now when war is surely over,
Rusting tanks will rest in clover.

And Patton, bless his soul, is gone.
Who are we to say it's wrong!
God took him when his time had come
And when his job was done.

CHAPTER 13:
CAMP GORDON BECOMES FORT GORDON, SIGNAL CENTER

By today's standards, the Signal Corps is flexible and far-reaching. By tomorrow's standards signals will be more swift and accurate, assessing situations and plugging into the chain of command to aid in decision-making.

Research to this end is continuing at Fort Gordon, where the Tenth Armored once trained and lived in basic barracks; where soldiers now learn the facets of a Signal Corps in modern surroundings. The country-club atmosphere is a far cry from the basics of 50 years ago, and belies the serious work being done.

Our veterans marvel at the action! Throughout this city of 16,000 you can see men training in earnest...running on the track, jogging in groups. Everywhere you turn, people are in command of groups in some kind of training. In addition to the 11,800 soldiers, 4,500 civilians help run the post.

At the Signal Corps Museum, the past is brought up to date in stages, with life-size dioramas on either side of a winding aisle. The mission of the U.S. Signal Museum and Fort Gordon Museum is to function as a permanent historical and educational institution at Fort Gordon, providing training and education to the soldiers, military dependents at Fort Gordon, and to the general population all aspects of the history of the Signal Corps, development of Fort Gordon and the vicinity, and the U.S. Army. The accuracy of the training and educational program is dependent upon proper collections, recording, conservation, and research of artifacts, pictures, and other historical documentary materials. The museum is also responsible for recommendations concerning preservation, protection, development, and enhancement of historical buildings, monuments, works, and sites throughout Fort Gordon Military Reservation. The museum serves as a medium of stimulating esprit de corps and advancing knowledge of the Signal Corps, Fort Gordon and the U.S. Army.

The museum offers one of the most complete and comprehensive collections of communication material in the United States. It includes signal devices from the Civil War such as wig-wag flags, developed by General Myer, a Beardsley Electro Magneto, and early keying mechanisms; as well as the sophisticated microwave equipment used during the Viet Nam conflict.

In world War II, the SCR-300 was effective for short distances, but heavier than today's units with their smaller batteries. It was deemed necessary to develop a hand-held radio that would carry farther than just across a river or field.

The BC-611 was the first truly portable hand-held radio, replacing the SCR-194. The SCR-300, page 133, was the one we were most familiar with.

The walkie-talkie plays an even greater role now than it did in World War II. Then, it was in a stage of infancy, and batteries were larger. Now it is much easier to carry! The future is limitless for this type of equipment. Battery inventions that have been held off the market will have to be unearthed so that the Armed Services will be able to send and receive over much greater distances without the use of wire. Smaller, more effective and longer lasting batteries will be the norm as we reach into the next century. It would be a shame of we found out that battery companies were promiscuously holding back from production after buying out important patents.

During World War II our 150th Armored Signal Company was always juicing-up the batteries for other units, including infantry divisions that fought alongside us. Consistently we would receive orders to furnish these back-pack SCR-300's by the dozen. I think some of these must have been new ones sent to us as the best way to dispense them to the front.

The 10th Armored Division, the 26th and the 4th Infantry Divisions trained at Camp Gordon (Now Fort Gordon). World War II items from these divisions are on display, including personal belongings of General Barton of the 4th Infantry, after whom Barton Field is named.

America was clearly brought into World War II on December 7, 1941 when the Japanese deliberately bombed Pearl Harbor. Two signalmen, Pvt. Joseph L. Lockard and Pvt. George A. Elliott were stationed at the North shore of Oahu, operating their radio aircraft-detection device, the SCR-270, which was very new and very secret. At 0702, Lockard and Elliott spotted an echo on the oscilloscope such as neither of them had ever seen. *(Continued on page 135.)*

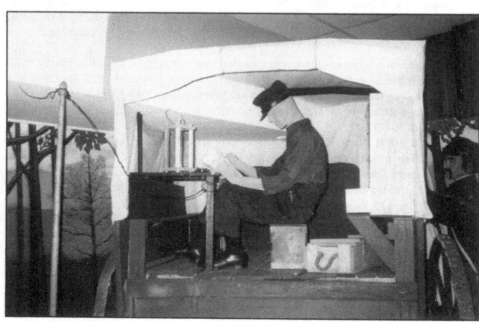

During the Civil War, communication by telegraph wire was of utmost importance, as evidenced by this life-size display.

A battery wagon of the Civil War era used for communications by telegraph.

WAC World War II.

A display at the Signal Corps Museum reminds me of World War II, although none of our Radio Operators were dummies! A meeting room at the museum is devoted to photographs and artwork of signaling and signal notables. Right: The soldier in the foreground is using a field phone like the one we used to shoot trouble on the line.

By their calculations, a large flight of airplanes was 132 miles off Kahuku Point and approaching at a speed of three miles a minute. At 0720, Lockard and Elliott called the information center at Fort Shafter where Pvt. Joseph P. McDonald received the call and told Lt. Kermit Tyler, who showed no interest. Lt. Tyler told Pvt. Lockard to "Forget it". The Japanese air attack began at 0755.

A half century ago, a forest of poles like the ones above faced us as wire recruits. Men have belted in on the first practice poles. Later, they will face the armless ones in the background, where lack of concentration could cause you to fall backward if you go too high before belting in!

Batteries replaced the hand-cranked radio used in early days of World War II while battery units were in their infancy. Soldier on the right is sending Morse Code on the set.

Realistic artwork of World War II tank battle confirms importance of commication. Helmets like these were carry-overs from World War I.

HISTORY OF EARLY COMMUNICATIONS
courtesy of the U.S. Army Signal Corps

Signals by means of torches, flags, smoke, pyrotechnics, and other symbols have been employed from time immemorial. But the systems of signaling were either difficult to learn or the equipment was cumbersome in form, complex in character, or impractical to manufacture on a scale large enough to be effective in mobile military operations.

The first section of the Signal museum begins with the development of sophisticated communications systems of the Greeks, Romans, and of the American Indians.

In late 1700's in France, Claude Chappe developed machines he called telegraphs. His telegraph system relied on visual signals by use of dials and pendulums. The telegraph system Chappe developed was successful during its time, as long as the weather permitted. The speed and distance at which a message could be transmitted at that time over a ten mile area was less than nine minutes!

During the Revolutionary War, the American Army used sword and drum codes to relay messages and to maneuver troops. On exhibit is a replica Revolutionary war uniform and a rifle and sabre from the period.

The last part of the section tells of Samuel Morse and his invention, the telegraph. Morse's telegraph was very different from Chappe's, as Morse's depended upon electricity, not visuals. The first telegraph line was opened in 1845 from Washington to Baltimore. The first message was "What hath God wrought'.

In 1858, just prior to the Civil War, a submarine cable spanning the Atlantic was laid by Cyrus W. Field. A piece of the original cable was presented to Chief Signal Officer Gibbs in 1931.

CIVIL WAR PERIOD 1861-1865

Crossed flags and torch, insignia of the Signal Corps, represent the first means of military communication employed by Albert James Myer, founder, organizer, and first chief of the United States Army Signal Corps. A collection of some of Albert J. Myer's personal belongings are the property of the Signal Corps Museum.

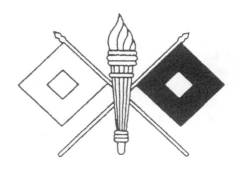

Myers genius lay in his ability to devise a simple visual signal system of "wigwagging" a flag by day and a torch by night to the right or left to indicate dots and dashes.

General Grant, shown at Kencsaw Mountain near Atlanta, with his observer and signalman.

A trained soldier can easily send and receive messages with this system, which met essential military requirements. It employed light, sturdy, easily transportable, easily-made equipment. Some Civil War signaling devices, ship-to-shore signaling equipment and some original issue wig-wag flags and telegraph keys are property of the Signal Corps Museum.

Albert J. Myer pressed for a separate branch of the Signal Corps. On June 21, 1860, the United States Congress authorized the army one signal officer with the rank of Major and $2,000.00 for signaling equipment. Myer, repeating his arguments for a separate Signal Corps, finally succeeded. On March 3, 1863, an act was passed providing a separate Signal Corps during the Civil War. The United States Army Signal Corps was born.

The Civil War was the first in the United States in which the electric telegraph was extensively employed during wartime, although there was no military telegraph organization at the outset of the war. The personnel of the U.S. Military Telegraph Company served as employees of the Quartermaster's Department, with no definite official standing. It was simply a civilian bureau made up of a few of the favored members, who received commissions. Myer tried in vain to absorb The Military Telegraph Company into the Signal Corps. His individual action was not appreciated by Secretary of War Stanton, who summarily dismissed Myer because of his insubordinate actions. A mock-up of a cipher disk used by Myer's signalmen may be seen, along with the telegraph key used by William Penn who at the age of 16 was a civilian employee for The Military Telegraph Company.

Balloons were also used on both sides during the Civil War. The Confederates had very little success with their balloons because of lack of materials. In July, 1861, Albert Myer asked for a "tethered" balloon. He realized the advantage an army would have in observing and directing artillery fire from up in a balloon. However, Myer ran into bad luck with his balloon. First, it arrived late and because it was tethered while being moved, it became torn to shreds on tree limbs on the way to the battle of Bull Run (Manassas). Professor Thaddeous Lowe did better with his balloons. Two in action with the Union Army were the "Enterprise" and "Intrepid." From the balloon "Enterprise" he sent the first airborne message...to President Lincoln. Lowe also provided General McClelland with valuable intelligence during the Peninsula and Chancellorsville campaigns in 1861.

The Confederate Signal Corps was formally established by the Confederate Congress on April 19, 1862 as a separate branch of the Confederate Army. This was almost a full year before the U.S. Congress established the U.S. Signal Corps as a separate branch. E.P. Alexander, whom Myer taught, organized the Confederate Signal Corps, the first independent branch of professional military signalmen.

The lack of skilled telegraph operators and the heavy batteries required to power the telegraphs created some problems in transportation. Invention of a hand-held magneto generator by G.W. Beardslee allowed it to be substituted for the heavy wet cells. Anyone who could read and write could operate the machine. The generator moved a dial indicator on the sending instrument, causing an index on the receiving machine to point to the designated letter.

The illustration is echoed in a display at the museum that represents both the "Flying Telegraph" and American Military Telegraph Battery Wagon. Wagons used to transport telegraph equipment had to carry 100 wet cell batteries which weighed over 1,000 pounds; and also had to carry five miles of telegraph wire. The telegraph lines could be set up at the rate of two miles per hour.

Signalmen of the U.S. Army were called upon to perform signaling duties anytime and anywhere day and night. It was necessary to devise a kit that could be used to carry the equipment. It had to be light, portable, easily packed and repacked for quick movement. Such a kit was constructed and a breakdown of the kit and signaling apparatus is on display at the museum.

Fort Gordon was named after the Confederate General John Brown Gordon, considered one of the bravest fighting men this country has ever known. He fought gallantly in many battles and was seriously injured on more than one occasion.

Robert E. Lee awarded General Gordon the sad honor of handing over the Army of Northern Virginia, in formal surrender, to General Joshua Chamberlain at Appomattox, to end the bloodiest war America has ever seen. Gordon went on to become a U.S. Senator. In 1889 he was elected Governor of the state of Georgia.

John Brown Gordon

THE AGE OF INVENTION
1865-1908

In its role as communicator for the Army and in its zeal to provide our troops with the most rapid and effective means of communications, the Signal Corps has always been quick to adopt, modify, and whenever necessary, to directly contribute to such inventions as the telegraph, telephone and radio. Wars have turned out to be the testing ground for such inventions.

During the period 1870-1890, under the leadership of Chief Signal Officer Myer, the Signal Corps organized and established the Meteorological Service. All phases of weather reporting were developed for the benefit of our nation's present day Weather Service...all

by the Signal Corps. By 1875, the Meteorological Service was so advanced that it comprised hundreds of stations from the Atlantic to the Pacific and in adjoining areas of Canada and the Caribbean.

This attracted the attention of weather people throughout the world. The U.S. War Dept., through the Signal Corps, was influential in establishing the first international cooperation in development of a worldwide meteorological service. General Myer remarked that benefits to be had for the weather service were "vast and lasting".

In 1881, signal officer Greely sailed to Lady Franklin Bay, Grinnell Sound, in the Artic. His mission was to establish the "Farthest North" outpost to record the weather conditions and phenomena in the Artic. Despite his hardships and tragedies, and the subsequent rescue of the expedition, all the scientific records were complete!

In 1890, the Signal Corps was reorganized in personnel and duties. The Weather Service became the Weather Bureau of the Department of Agriculture.

LT. GREELY

Eight years later the United States found itself in a war with Spain. The war extended to Cuba, Puerto Rico and the Philippines. At this early stage there were only eight officers and 52 enlisted men in the Signal Corps, with a budget of $800. The Corps was reorganized with a Volunteer Corps in order to provide the rapidly expanding Army with communications. To a greater extent than any other corps in the Army, the Signal Corps operations and sphere of usefulness was expanded by the Spanish American War.

THE WAR WITH SPAIN brought to use the first telephones by the Signal Corps. It was also the first time in history a direct telephone line was established between the President of the United States in Washington, D.C., and the battle front in Santiago, Cuba. Telephones were installed from the headquarters of Generals Wheeler and Kent, near San Juan Hill.

By 1912 the United States once again found itself in a conflict, this time with the Mexican bandit Pancho Villa, who was crossing the Mexican border into American territory raiding, robbing and killing Americans. Field companies "D" and "I" were placed on Mexican border duty in 1912. The next year companies "B" and "H" were organized and assigned to similar service. Service Buzzer lines were installed between the outposts and headquarters of the expeditionary force to six different points in the city of Vera Cruz in 1914. Maximum wire mileage was approximately 300 miles, with about a dozen stations South of the border. (In 1944 the 10th Armored signalmen ran over 300 miles of wire in three days at the battle of Metz.) Radio service was supplementary to the buzzer traffic, which was very heavy. Radio pack sets were in use, and radio tractors were employed for the first time.

SIGNAL CORPS AVIATION
1908-1917

The success of the Wright Brothers aeroplane led to the formation of the Aeronautical Division in the Signal Corps. The first aeroplanes purchased by the U.S. Army were for the Signal Corps.

In 1907, specifications were prepared and proposals invited for a heavier-than-air machine, speed 40 miles per hour, to remain in the air one hour, under control. A.M. Herring and the Wright Brothers competed for the contract. The Wright Brothers won.

Two men who had become firsts in the history of aviation were Lt. Thomas E. Selfridge and Lt. Frederic E. Humphreys. Lt. Selfridge, on the afternoon of Septem-

Telegraph Station in the Philippine Islands, 1899.

LT. SELFRIDGE

LT. HUMPHREYS

ber 17, 1908, was flying with Orville Wright at the controls when the airplane crashed from a height of 150 ft. Selfridge was the first person to be killed in an airplane accident. On October 26, 1909, Lt. Humphreys was given three hours of flight instruction by Wilber Wright and became the first Army officer to fly solo later that day.

In 1911, the first Army Aviation School was opened at College Park, Maryland, moving to Augusta, Georgia, during the Winter. In 1912, aerial photographs were taken and radio air-to-ground communication was performed.

The Aeronautical Division of the Signal Corps had been set up in 1907 with its new chief Captain Charles de F. Chandler. His first project was to establish a Balloon Detachment at Fort Omaha. Ballooning was a couple of years ahead of the airplane at that time. In July of 1908, Dirigible No. 1 was delivered to Fort Myer. Its first flight lasted for seven minutes and attained a maximum altitude of 250 feet. In later trials it flew for two hours and reached a top speed at 19.6 miles per hour.

The act of July 18, 1914, Authorized an Aviation Section of the Signal Corps. Available air resources of the Army were put at the disposal of the Punitive Expedition into Mexico in 1916. However, the high altitudes and dry atmosphere caused propeller difficulties and the few machines on hand were rapidly "used up".

WORLD WAR I
1917-1919

The use of signal communication in WWI was extensive and the tasks of the Signal Corps varied. Some of the tasks were: radio, telephone, photographic, pigeon and other special services. Balloons were used. Their function was to regulate artillery fire, locate targets, report all activity seen within the enemy lines by day, and to report all that could be seen at night.

During WWI, General "Black Jack" Pershing asked for female volunteers to operate the telephone switchboards in France. The women had to meet certain requirements. They had to be single, college educated and speak French. Over 200 female operators served in France for the Signal Corps. They became known as "Hello Girls". Their service proved so valuable and of such importance that it led to the formation of the Women's Army Corps.

The Pigeon Service did not exist in the American Army prior to WWI. Experiments on the Mexican border were unsuccessful due to the inexperience of the personnel handling the birds. The Chief Signal Officer of the American Expeditionary Force recommended the establishment of a Pigeon Service as a branch of the Signal Corps. The use of Pigeons was then quite successful. In the Meuse-Argonne offensive, a total of 442 American birds were used for about 400 messages.

Photography was divided into two sections, ground and aerial. Ground photography, including that for historical use and news purposes, was assigned to the Signal Corps in 1917. Ground photography was subdivided into still and motion picture. Aerial photography was of primary use to the Intelligence Service.

The Radio Intelligence Service established listening posts in "No Man's Land" for the purpose of picking up enemy messages. The posts were located in trenches, where experienced operators sat at their instruments. The use of radio was subject to frequent interruptions and suspension of service. Radio apparatus was often damaged in transportation and great difficulty was experienced in maintaining the supply of storage batteries. Radio worked better from division headquarters to the rear than within the division.

THE INTERWAR YEARS
1920 - 1941

The Army between the two world wars labored on the development of the highly secret Radar. Colonel William R. Blair holds the fundamental and basic patent for American Radar.

It became necessary to replace the Washington-Alaska cable, laid at the beginning of the 1900's. During this period, every word of press dispatch news from the outside world came into Alaska over the Signal Corps wire system.

Two important additional photographic activities were undertaken. First, the Signal Corps was charged with the production, distribution and storage of Army training films. The second new activity was pictorial publicity.

The War Department Message Center was organized in 1923 under the direct control of the Chief Signal Officer. It was charged with handling War Department traffic to points outside Washington and such business as it may receive from other government sources. Radio and wire telegraph were the principal agencies, supplemented by cable, telephone, and messenger.

The invention and development of the electron tube was judged by the Signal Corps as one of primary importance. Electron tubes are the very heart of countless pieces of

Signal Corps equipment. This is changing as time goes on.

Frequency Modulation (FM) radio sets were developed by the Signal Corps Laboratories in cooperation with the radio industry a full three years before Pearl Harbor. FM radio sets offered crystal clear reception without static. Severe ignition interference is circumvented with very little power consumption at greater distances than AM radio sets.

VIETNAM AND BEYOND

In the mid-1960's the AN/TSC-79SHF "team pack" was developed. It was one of six configurations of small, portable satellite communications ground terminals for use in the joint-service TACSATCOM I experimental test program. One of the forerunners of today's highly transportable and flexible Ground Mobile Forces TACSATCOM terminals was the TSC-79. The 79 set up in 15 minutes.

An experimental helmet radio, the AN/PRC34(X1) was intended for squad communications. It was designed in the late 1950's and tested throughout 1960, but was not adopted by the Army. It might have been good for "tankers" but was adopted instead by football teams. Objections cancelled out this use, however.

In 1964, signal advisors in Vietnam had discovered the PRC-25 to be more advantageous than the PRC-10. The 25 could transmit over a greater distance in the dense jungle. It was easier to find a clear frequency and could operate over a far greater frequency span. General C.W. Abrams Jr. considered the AN/PRC-25 to be the single most important tactical item used in Vietnam by the U.S. Army.

One of the regulations of the Hanoi Hilton, the old French prison in Hanoi, was number 10: "Criminals must not communicate with or look at other criminals in other rooms or outside." One way the prisoners communicated was by a tap code. The tap code was a secret code that could be used

147

by tapping on walls, coughing, or pounding out on the ground. Other clandestine methods of communication within the POW compound were hiding messages in loaves of bread, scratching notes on bottoms of plates or leaving messages written with homemade ink at pre-determined locations. The American POW's were subject to torture if the messages were ever discovered. However, the need for any tidbits about the States became food for starving minds. Even remote fellowship with other Americans brought comfort.

UNUSUAL COMMUNICATIONS

During World War I and II the Army had favorable experience in using Native American Indians as signal soldiers. The Army was afraid the Germans and Japanese might break our code, so Indians were used as "Code Talkers." These signalmen came from such tribes as the Choctaw, Comanche and Sioux.

Two SCR-271 antennas used side-by-side proved for the first time that man could communicate by electronic means through outer space. In 1958, President Eisenhower sent a Christmas message of peace over the Score satellite, first voice relay satellite sent into space by America.

U.S. ARMY SOUTHEASTERN SIGNAL SCHOOL
from the Fort Gordon Story 1941-1964

The United States Army Southeastern Signal School is one of the finest technical schools in the U.S. Army and has expanded to become the largest activity devoted to the training of soldiers in the fields of installation, operation, and maintenance of modern signal equipment.

Since its activation on October 25, 1948, the USASESCS has become a complex training school, closely resembling a civilian technical school or a communications college. The ever-increasing demands of the modern Army for communications-electronics specialists has caused the initial graduating class of 10 students to grow into a weekly output of more than 400 newly graduated Signal Corps technicians.

The organization of the Southeastern Signal School consists of the Office of the Commandant; the Program and Budget Officer; Office of the Secretary; Officer of Logistics; Director of Instruction, and the Troop Command. The Troop Command is composed of four battalions with a total of 29 companies and is responsible for the housing, feeding and military training of students attending any one of the 19 MOS courses in the school.

The Director of Instruction is responsible for the training of the students in the MOS to which they are assigned. The instructional areas are divided into three departments of Communications: Basic, Radio and Wire.

An Officer Department was added in April 1961 which is responsible for conducting

Some historical Signal Corps equipment is on display at the Patton Museum at Fort Knox, such as this official Signal Truck outfitted with lighted interior, sending and receiving set. A generator was used to complement the batteries.

the Signal Officer Basic Course, a nine week course in basic communications for newly commissioned Signal Corps officers. The course trains more than 1,100 new Signal Corps officers yearly. Signal Corps training at Fort Gordon dates back to October 1, 1958 when the Signal Corps Training Center was established at then Camp Gordon as a Class II activity under the control of the Chief Signal Officer, Department of the Army.

The USASESCS claims the world's largest closed-circuit educational television installation which daily beams lectures, demonstrations and technical instruction over 14 channels to its many thousands of students. The network consists of 221-2 miles of co-axial cable; and some 400 hours of instructions are aired each week from the main studio. The program was initiated at Fort Gordon in October, 1961.

OTHER SCHOOLS LOCATED AT FORT GORDON:
U.S. Army Military Police School
U.S. Army Civil Affairs School

MAJOR UNITS LOCATED AT FORT GORDON:
4th Army Postal Unit
18th Surgical Hospital
88th Military Police Detachment
95th Civil Affairs Group
41st Civil Affairs Company
42nd Civil Affairs Company
140th Military Police Company
167th Signal Company (radio relay, very high frequency)
299th Engineer Battalion (Combat - Army)
434th AG Army Band
593rd Signal Company (CCO)
U.S. Army Combat Developments Command Civil Affairs Agency
U.S. Army Combat Developments Command Military Police Agency
WAC Company

FORT KNOX
Fort Knox is frequented by servicemen and veterans, especially of the Armored Divisions. The general public is also drawn to the museum, to a total of over 300,000 per year! The most impressive feature of the Museum of Cavalry and Armor is the large array of tanks, inside and out that comprise this extensive collection.

In addition to U.S. tanks of awesome size, small Japanese tanks and deadly low-slung German tanks are displayed: Panther, Tiger and King Tiger...and the Soviet T34. You can look into a U.S. Patton tank and a German King Tiger, both with their interior views sided with plexiglass.

By 1945, tanks with larger bogy wheels and cannon having greater velocity were being produced. One of these from the Tenth Armored "Tiger" Division is on display outside the museum. Note the painted tiger on the front (see previous page).

*History is complete when a diorama shows
a maintenance crew installing a new engine
in a tank under battlefield conditions, like
men of our 132nd Ordnance Battalion.*

CHAPTER 14
COAST PROTECTION

There were many servicemen and servicewomen working on the home front, some at jobs that were kept secret from the general public. There was a team on the West coast just checking on balloons that the Japanese were sending over to lay waste to our timber industry. Surprisingly enough, our reporters, and the editors they worked for, kept this story under wraps so the Japanese would not know that their fire bomb balloons were enjoying a moderate rate of success. If they had known how many landed, they would have released hundreds more. As it was, most of them caused only a little amount of damage.

Almost every shipping harbor had surveillance personnel that worked round-the-clock...on the alert for invasion by saboteur teams. Merchant ships plying the Atlantic coast were having a tough time against the German subs, but we fought back with fast patrol boats. After a while we got the upper hand, but for a period we were losing many ships.

"German U-boats would lay off the northern end of the Florida straits waiting for oil tankers from Texas to come up the coast," said Al McCulloch, Radar man. Al was a Petty Officer 3rd Class, on patrol with his 86-ft. PCS (Patrol Craft Escort - Submarines). "Our ship was all-wood with twin diesel engines, each delivering 1,100 H.P. Armaments were 30 and 50-caliber machine guns, plus depth charges. Our 250-lb. rear depth charges rolled off, so we had to be going at a good rate of speed. After they exploded, we would sweep coral and fish off the rear deck," emphasized McCulloch. "We also had Hedge Hog depth charges of only 50-lbs. that were fired off the bow like mortars...200 to 400 feet!

"One of our patrol boats captured a German sub in the straits, between Cuba and the Florida Keys. The captain had to surrender, because it wasn't deep enough to evade the depth charges. Seams were splitting and the sub had to come up to the surface."

Other than shipboard, Radar was being used for coast protection. In Europe, these towering units faced toward land, from which enemy planes were expected, heading for the build-up and supplies at beaches and docks.

You can see by this illustration that it was a set-up that could be set up in a hurry. The one shown here is similar to the one in use at Hawaii. Normally, two trucks would be used; one for the operator to watch for blips that defined enemy planes. Our planes were furnished with a system that emitted a second blip, which identified them.

There were large bunkers with big-bore cannon facing the ocean to try to get a bead on enemy ships several miles out at sea. Looking around 50 years later, it was only those that were in use in one way or another that were not too overgrown with trees and weeds. On Sullivan Island, near Charleston, South Carolina, two of these bunkers were made into all-weather homes - easy to heat.

Some bunkers were not so pretentious. This one near Fort Fisher, North Carolina, was the training ground for

Robert E. Harrell. (By Fred Pickler.)

troops that attacked it, not from the sea, but from the land. Live ammunition would be fired from machine gun slots in the side. It was excellent training for soldiers learning to keep their heads down under fire. Usually men would incur the wrath of the sergeant as he shouted, "Keep your butts down, you'll look funny in a butt sling!" I never heard anyone laugh at that one while crawling under live fire!

A man lived and died in this abandoned bunker. Known as the Hermit of Fort Fisher, he was well liked. Robert E. Harrell had the gift of gab...so people who came from miles around didn't feel strange to intrude. They came to visit; to talk, to listen, to observe; and they left with the feeling that he was happy living there. He was where he wanted to be.

Inside, living was easy. He didn't have to clean up if he didn't want to. He had one worry. Teen age boys would pick on him.

Fred Pickler, a police evidence reporter, stayed with the hermit for a week, camping

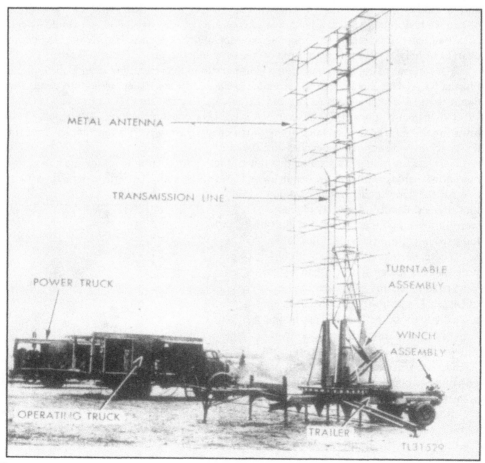

METAL ANTENNA

TRANSMISSION LINE

POWER TRUCK

TURNTABLE ASSEMBLY

WINCH ASSEMBLY

OPERATING TRUCK

TRAILER

TL31579

These bunkers on Sullivan's Island were converted to roomy abodes and decked out with two-story pillared entrances.

out to see if he was all right. "For seven days I lived in a tent down by his bunker to do research for an article on the hermit for the local paper; and to see if he was all right," Pickler said. "There was a report that some teenagers were harassing the hermit. Sure enough, it happened while I was about to go to sleep in a tent I had pitched near his bunker. I could hear their voices," related Pickler. "One of them said, 'The hermit has a tent; let's drag him down by the marsh!' When I heard that, I shined my flashlight on them, pointed my 45 so they could see it, and one of them said 'He has a gun- let's get out of here!' They left in a hurry before I could get a good look at them. Coincidently, the hermit was killed the same way, another time. He was probably dragged or carried down to the marsh, where his sleeping bag cover was found. It looked like he had tried to escape and had a heart attack."

These teenagers are grown men now, but have to live with what they have done. Their object, to harass an old man, was murder. Over $2,000 in coins was found in the rubble, but it was not hidden treasure. It was the product of caring people who left tips for the hermit to better his life.

CHAPTER 15

ARMOR TECHNIQUES OF GREAT GENERALS

As Rommel was the father of armored forces in Germany, so Patton was assuredly the originator in the United States. My research leads me to believe there were three ways to use armor. Most of our generals understood the German Blitzkrieg to mean that armor would lead an attack, followed by an entire army, or corps. Usually, it would be preceded by an extensive artillery barrage and would proceed to a designation in a straight or curved line. The second method, also using artillery and bombers to soften up the enemy, would be used to make a breakthrough at the front, but most generals would not carry it forward for fear of flank attacks, until armies or divisions on the flank could be brought up. This method, which Monty used effectively, was slower. It also drew more opposition, because it gave the enemy time to move troops into a defensive position. It gave the appearance of moving against great odds. Really what it was doing was telegraphing intention to the opposition.

You can determine by the actions of various armored divisions under Patton's command that a third use of armor was beginning to develop. Our Tenth Armored Division is a case in point! When we broke through, it was not unusual to be cut off and still attacking. Patton's armor was not told to wait 'til the infantry divisions caught up, yet they contributed extensively to our successes. Patton's armor would go in different directions, many times leaving the infantry to clear a city that impeded our progress. Others cast snide remarks at this technique, but why is it that the Germans count Patton as our best general? They knew not where to bring up troops to block us, so it looked to others (up in Monty Land?) like resistance amounted to nil.

At Trier, we knocked at the door, then went around the back door and our tanks captured a bridge intact. At Kaiserslautern the defense was tougher and it became a harder nut to crack. The 80th Infantry Division was used to rid the city of enemy troops. The enemy became confused. The 10th Armored, no longer defending, came tearing out of the city, attacking.

Patton's method was to always attack...straight ahead, to the left or right; sometimes even to the rear. But never to the rear in the same direction. His method could be likened to a chess player who gets his bishop out amongst the opposition, protected only by the rook. At this point he brings up his knight, in case the bishop is cut off from the rook's protection. The other chess player is forced to move from the path of the bishop, and it attacks in a different direction, taking a "piece."

This is the third method of using armor. When a division breaks through the line, or front, an armored division is rushed to the breach, followed of course by a couple of infantry divisions. If another armored division is available, it should follow immediately. If not, the first one through the line keeps going until it meets resistance it cannot handle alone. By that time an infantry division is certain to catch up. If they both stay there and beat their infantry on the defences of a city, the enemy could bring up reinforcements to their detriment. If the armored division stalks away in a different direction it forces the enemy to focus on where our strength is, and try to offset it. At that time our main strength could be coming up toward the city in question, but it can't be set upon too heavily by the enemy troops because of the unknown or flexible location of the fast-moving armored division.

If the elusive armored division is to one side of the city in question, it is certainly a danger to the enemy. It could move around in back of the city as our main attack comes up; or it could move to the side, thus endangering any enemy attempt to push against that flank of our main attack coming through the hole. Patton had us move to the side to attack!

I think most of our generals like to, as Monty would say, "Tidy up their front." Maybe it would be better to have an uneven front, not just by mistake, with opportunities to throw fear at the enemy.

These pages are designed to reflect on famous men. All great wars contain blunders. This one had its share. The quirks of even our best generals also prove their undoing, sometimes not only in battle.

Napoleon, whom Montgomery emulated, met his fate at the battle of Waterloo, and was banished to an island. Rommel failed twice: once when he took a day off to see his family, allowing our armies to come ashore; a second time when he was drawn into the Hitler assassination plot, ending his career. He did not make a mistake at the battle of El Alemain, he just lost the battle to Monty's preparedness. This was one of the truly great battles that changed the course of the war in our favor.

Montgomery's worst enemy was his mouth. So was Patton's. Each of these men ached to do more of the planning. Both were well qualified, and could have helped Eisenhower in the planning stage, but they were used to observing the battle because they reveled in it. Montgomery always wanted more than his share of the credit, and got it with his many pronouncements to the press. Finally, he wrote to Eisenhower, asking for his command to lead the major assault. This would have entailed use of our armor and men, with Monty getting all the credit. He was put in his place with a polite letter from Ike.

Even when Eisenhower accepted a suggestion to appoint Montgomery as temporary commander of forces in the Northern sector during the Bulge, he used this to garner more credit for himself. Eisenhower was looking at the big picture - a possible disruption of communication lines. Montgomery bragged that he was asked to save the situation.

Patton was even less diplomatic than Monty. He swore a lot. He wanted more of the action, and could also have run away with the whole show! He went to Eisenhower, whom he knew personally, and asked to be allowed to go forward, and was turned down.

Patton was more "right" than Montgomery, in my estimation. Montgomery would have had to use U.S. armor, and commit them to battle ahead of U.K. troops, as he did with the 7th Armored when he was given temporary command of our army in the North. He would have then taken credit for the whole operation, as he did with his temporary assignment.

Actually, Patton's Third Army cut off the Panzer onslaught, while Montgomery languished, studying his maps. Many Germans escaped this trap, but their armies were decimated, some never again organized.

If Patton had been allowed to go ahead with an armored thrust in his sector, and given enough gas, who knows how soon the war might have ended! The northern sector, where Montgomery wanted to expand, had a February thaw. In addition, Germans had flooded much of the maneuverable land, which did slow down our armor. Then, based on how fast we went in the southern sector once General Patton was unleashed, this could have been the way to go.

Truly, Montgomery and Patton were both great generals, and Eisenhower had to treat them with kid gloves - up to a point. Montgomery had the last laugh. He outlived both

Rommel and Patton, the two best tank experts in World War II, and now, 50 years later, English authors, researching General Montgomery's press releases, have given their beloved Monty much more than his share of the credit.

Another great Allied General of World War II was DeGaulle. He came forward to represent the Free French when others held back, thinking that Germany might win. DeGaulle had character. He stood up for what he believed. The United States recognized his worth and gave him well-justified support. When our troops were about to by-pass Paris he asked for our help. The plan wasn't changed until French began fighting in the streets, then we sent in a French division to clear the city; and had our 28th Division march through on their way to battle!

This gave DeGaulle the recognition he needed. He was the up-and-coming political figure of the day; just the one needed to lead the independent French nation.

If the glory of battle was not so much in the minds of our generals, we might have fewer wars. But, to be effective, it is important for them to instill this desire in the minds of their men. Therein lies our dilemma. A general is a student of war. It is important to him to put his studies into action. Patton put his action where his mouth was. Montgomery put his mouth where his action was. Eisenhower tempered his actions and got the job done. DeGaulle stepped forward at the right time. They were excellent generals.

The best general may have been George S. Patton. We will never know for sure, but to study his war room and the men who ran it gives us an indication. For instance, Sgt. Dave Clark, senior N.C.O. in Patton's War Room was selected for his multiple abilities: mechanical engineering, draftsmanship, stenography. He would help with both flat battle maps and terrain relief maps. "We would send up planes to take photos, then piece them together and make terrain maps to precise measurements," Clark said. "At Metz we made terrain maps of every one of those forts, and pooled information as it came in. Col. Carter would read books on earlier battles, and it was one of these that gave us valuable hints on how to attack.

"There were several men attached to Third Army Headquarters that brought back information from behind enemy lines. Dressed like peasants, they would take chances to find weak spots between the German divisions."

Clark spoke about two one-star generals that Patton had on his staff: General Koch and Harry Maddox, G3 - operations, both of whom were with Patton in Africa. They were both top men, and worked long hours to help the Third Army. "When we were getting ready to go into battle in Europe," Clark confirmed, "Patton would hear about a new piece of equipment the English were working on, and he would assign someone to check it out, saying 'Go over and see what their new toy is.'

"Patton's presence was felt when the Third Army first went into action. He ran off my map three times in one day. I was using a one-inch to 50-miles detailed map. When we got close to the city of Nancy I heard him talking on the phone to one of the generals: 'Ham. George. I want you to take Nancy tomorrow. I know you're running out of gas, but get there!'

"Our Third Army Headquarters became like a family. We would not have to salute inside, just say 'sir.' We had a constant work ethic. Neckties had to be worn, except during the Bulge, when we worked 'til exhausted, then waked the next man. We affectionately called General Patton 'Gentle George,' but never to his face.

"Our information on the Bulge build-up was up to date, and Patton told Eisenhower several times that something was up, but was ignored."

This treatment had an effect on the way history was written. Many historians are

English, bred in their great universities. In addition, American students of combat take battle technique courses in a prestigious English university. They ignore Patton, possibly because they find it hard to contend with his salty language.

It is hard to say which branch of the service contributed more to winning the war. I think the ones where men had the toughest time, day-to-day, like the infantry, Army and Marines alike, should get the most credit. My idea of armor's part in the war is only to explain how flexible use of armor may have shortened the war on the ground. Air corps certainly did more than they were asked to do, but pilots came back to warm quarters, and didn't experience the mud. Sailors had it tough during attack, although their cramped space was comfortable enough when they got a chance to rest.

Front line troops who slept in a hole they had to dig in frozen ground or in steaming jungle had it the worst. When they held the line they contributed the most.

There are exceptions. For instance, Seabees in foxholes with the infantry; an artillery observer, who stays with the infantry for days and nights during a battle; engineers who stand in cold water under fire to build bridges over one river after another, ceaselessly. You may think of several more. When I think of men who understood how rough the troops had it I think of Ernie Pyle, whose words let us all know how it was.

When the war ended I was glad to be well, and to have enough points to make it home by Christmas, 1945, and I gave...

THANKS
This prayer is, Lord, in retrospect;
We thank Thee, God, for time that's past -
For thoughts that in our minds reflect
A beauty that we hope will last.

The thoughts that will remain within;
We pray, are only those that stand
Defiant 'gainst the slightest sin
And stalwart in the strife-torn land.

Many men have lost their way
Among temptation's toillessness.
We realize and pause to pray,
And give our thanks for happiness.

We pray our thoughts will not be marred
By broken word or devilish glee.
Instead, we want our future starred;
Religion helping us to see.

We thank Thee for the gift of faith,
And hope it shall continue thus;
To lead the men of every race,
And be to all, life's omnibus.

Please heed our prayer, Oh Lord, today,
For sick and needy, whether home

Or wounded in the battle's fray -
Or lying in some foreign loam.

We pray for soul and spirit, too -
For friends who've left their earthly sphere,
And as for us, God keep us true,
Endow us with good health and cheer.

Don Young

When I was discharged, what had been a big event in the life of our country was coming to a close. Two years, nine months and three days had gone by since I became eligible for Army pay, thanks to a letter from Franklin D. Roosevelt.

CREDITS

Buddies from the 150th for material, photos, encouragement (150th Armored Signal Co., 10th Armored Div.) Frank Armbruster, Bob Anderson, Jim Hilton, Hoby Reed

Bill Boyan	Cover Material	(John Hancock Insurance Co.)
Bob Cassel	Research Material	(94th Infantry Div.)
Dave Clarke	Insights	(Sgt. Patton's War Room)
James Clark	Insights	(Sgt. Signal Corps, Patton's HQs)
Fred Crismon	Repro Work	(Photographer, Irvington, Ky.)
Don DiMarco	Artillery info, Artwork	(390th F.A. Bn., 78th Div.)
Susan Doorlay	Photos	Reading, PA.
Dave Eldridge	Battle Account /Marketing Strategy	Eldridge Ad agency
Marino S. Endrizzi	Battle Account	(90th Recon, 10th Armored)
Becky Greaves	Photos	(Ohio State Univ. Archives)
Roger Grigson	Interviews	(Volunteer, Chester Cty. Historical Society)
Earle Hart	Use of his Bulge Museum	(87th Infantry Div.)
John Hemsher	Battle Accounts	(741st Tank Bn.)
Ken Higbie	Production Advice	Ft. Myers, FL.
Frank Houston	Battle Information	(Hq3 Tenth Armored)
Glenn S. Jones	Research Material	(90th Recon, 10th Armd.)
Buddy Lovette	Photos, Suggestions	(165 Signal Photo Co.)
Robert Martin	Editorial Advice	(Turner Publishing Co., Paducah, Ky.)
Lothar Miller	Battle Account	(10th Armd.)
Jim Ortoleva	Photo, Tech. Advice	(45th Infantry Div.)
Erik Parrent	Editorial Follow-Up	(Turner Publishing Co., Paducah, Ky.)
Fred Pickler	Photos, History	(Photographer, Wilmington, N.C.)
John Purdy	Photos, Insights	(Director, Patton Museum, Ft. Knox)
Mrs. Hugh Rafferty	"Letters to Mom"	(from Hugh, 101st Airborne)
John Richardson	Battle Accounts	(80th Infantry Div.)
Herb Ridyard	Battle Accounts	(94th Infantry Div.)
Mike Rodgers and Museum Director Ted Wise	Photo Copies and Signal Corps History	(Signal Corps. Museum, Fort Gordon, GA.)
Julie Shea	Photo Copy	(Mobil Corp.)
Katie Talbot	Photos, Research	(Librarian, Patton Museum, Fort Knox, KY.)
Bill Wallace	Photo, Battle Account	(42nd Infantry Div.)
George Williams	Battle Accounts	(26th Infantry Div.)
Ruth Young	Encouragement, patience	

RESEARCH MATERIAL

Bastogne the Road Block, by Peter Elstob, Ballantine's Illus. Battle History of World War II, Ballantine Books, Inc., 1968 (Printed in U.S.A.)

The Battle for Germany, by H.E. Essame, Charles Scribner's Sons, N.Y. (Printed in Great Britain)

The Battle of the Bulge, by John Toland, Random House, N.Y. (Mfg. in the U.S.)

Crusade in Europe, by Dwight D. Eisenhower, Doubleday & Co. Inc., 1948, Garden City, N.Y. (Printed in the U.S.)

Ernie's War, by Ernie Pyle, Simon & Shuster, Inc., Edited by David Nichols, New York, 1987 (Printed in the U.S.)

Farewell to Valley Forge, by David Taylor, J.P. Lippincott Co., 1955 (Phila. & N.Y.)

Growl of the Tiger, by Dean M. Chapman, Turner Publishing, 1993 (Printed in the U.S.)

The Home Front USA, by A.A. Hoehling, Thomas Y. Crowell Co., N.Y. (Vail-Ballou Press, Inc., Binghamton, N.Y.)

History of World War II, Ed. Michael Wright , The Readers Digest Assn. Ltd., London (Printed in the U.S.)

Impact, by Lester M. Nichols, Bradbury, Sayles, O'Neill Co. Inc., 1954 (Printed in U.S.)

Life's Picture History of World War II, Ed. Arthur Tourtellot, Time Incorporated, N.Y.

The Modern U.S. Army, Ed. Richard O'Neill, Prentice Hall Press, N.Y., 1986 (Orig. printed in the UK)

Patton, by Charles Whiting, Ballantine's Illus. Battle History of World War II, 1970

The Patton Papers, by Martin Blumenson, Houghton Mifflin Co., 1974 (Boston)

Patton's Third Army, by Charles M. Province, Hippocrene Books, N.Y., 1992 (Printed in the U.S.A.)

The Pictorial History of World War II, by Charles Messenger, W.H. Smith Publishers Inc., N.Y. (Produced by Bison Books Corp., Greenwich, CT.)

NTC: A Primer of Modern Land Combat, by Hans Halberstadt, Presidio Press, Novato, CA, 1989

Roosevelt and Churchill: Their Secret Wartime Correspondence, Edited by Francis L. Loewenheim, Harold D. Langley, Manfred Jonas, Saturday Review Press, E.P. Dutton & Co., Inc., 1975 (Printed in the U.S.)

Scorched Earth, by Paul Carell (translation by Ewald Osers), Verlag, Ullstein GMBH, Frankfurt, Germany, Little, Brown & Co., Inc., Boston (1966, translation 1970)

United States Airborne Forces, by Leroy Thompson, Blanford Press, 1986, Dorset

The Unknown Patton, by Charles M. Province, Bonanza Books, N.Y., 1983

War As I Knew It, by General George S. Patton, Jr., Houghton Mifflin Co. Boston (Riverside Press, Cambridge)

The World Book Encyclopedia, Field Enterprises Educational Corp.

World War II, by Robert Hoare, Macdonald Educational Ltd., London (Morrison and Gibb Ltd.)

BATTLE HISTORIES

10th Armored Division Turner Publishing (Printed in U.S.)

150th Armored Signal Co. Battle Reports (U.S. Govt. Archives)

78th Infantry Division Ed. by T4 Miles Cahn & Pfc. James Friedman, Infantry Journal, Inc. (Washington, D.C.)

371st Tank Battalion Battle Reports

Third Army - A Brief History of Operations in Europe 301st Signal Bn., Reproduced by 652nd Eng. Bn.

History of Company "A" 309th Artillery Bn., Ed. by Sgt. Robert A. Brown, Printed by Buckman (Munich, Germany)

History of the 94th Ed. by Lt. Laurence G. Byrnes, Infantry Journal Press, 1948 (Washington, D.C.)

94th Infantry Division Commemorative Taylor Publishing (Dallas, Texas)

Patton's U.S. Army Training Booklet Desert Training Center (U.S. Army)

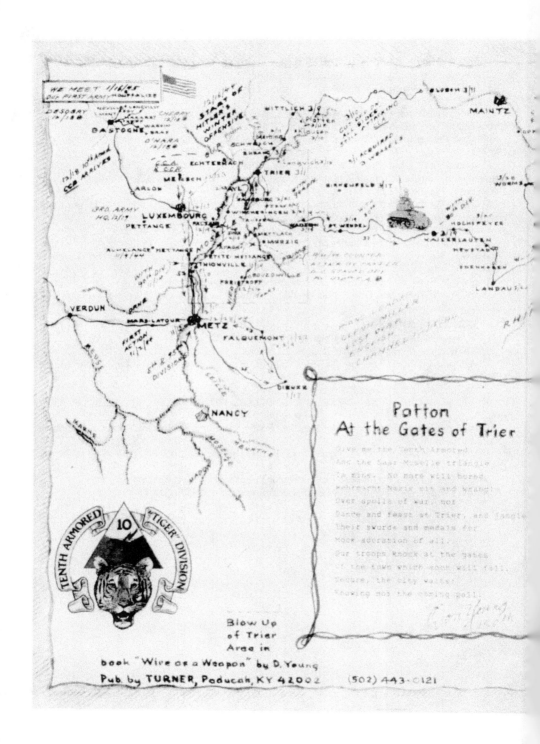

Patton
At the Gates of Trier

Give me the Tenth Armored
And the Saar-Moselle triangle
Is mine. No more will horned
Wehrmacht Nazis sin and wrangle
Over spoils of war, nor
Dance and feast at Trier, and jangle
Their swords and medals for
Mock adoration of all.
Our troops knock at the gates
Of the town which soon will fall.
Secure, the city waits
Knowing not the coming pall.

Blow Up
of Trier
Area in

book "Wire as a Weapon" by D. Young

Pub. by TURNER, Paducah, KY 42002   (502) 443-0121

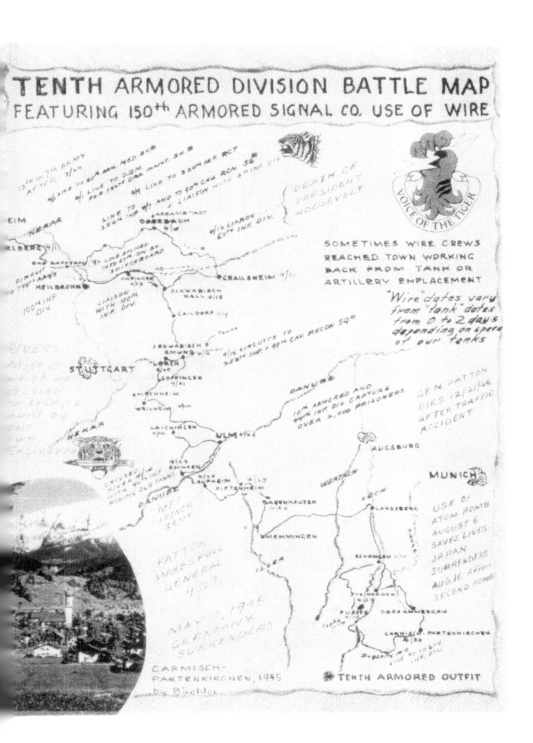

TENTH ARMORED DIVISION BATTLE MAP
FEATURING 150th ARMORED SIGNAL CO. USE OF WIRE

INDEX

Printed in the USA
CPSIA information can be obtained
at www.ICGtesting.com
LVHW091258150824
788261LV00005B/85

9 781563 112836